I Married the
KLONDIKE

I Married the

KLONDIKE

Laura Beatrice Berton

McClelland and Stewart

In Memory of Frank

The Canadian Publishers
McClelland and Stewart Limited
25 Hollinger Road
Toronto M4B 3G2

Film edition 1982
ISBN 0-7710-1230-6

Second printing 1982

Manufactured in Canada by Webcom Limited

The front cover shows Leueen Willoughby as Laura
and R.H. Thomson as Frank Berton in the CBC television
drama of I **Married the Klondike**.

Introduction to the New Edition

My mother was always writing. She came by it honestly for her father, Phillips Thompson, was a respected journalist and editor—a one-time associate of J. W. Bengough on *Grip*, a founder of a political weekly, *The National*, a contributor to *The Moon* and *American Punch*, a reporter for the *Toronto News*, the *Telegraph*, and the *Mail and Empire*, a leading light in the press galleries at Queen's Park and Ottawa and a columnist and later foreign correspondent for *The Globe*. I remember him in his last years working away at a roll-top desk in his study in Oakville, Ontario, as I remember my mother, scribbling away on the dining room table in our home in Dawson City and my father, pecking out the result for her on an old Underwood upright.

Before I was born she was sending dispatches out to *Saturday Night* and *The Family Herald* and when I was a small boy she wrote regularly for the *Dawson News*. I can remember taking her copy down to the office on Third Avenue on my CCM bicycle and watching Harold Malstrom, who was printer, editor, advertising man and circulation manager combined, setting it up on the linotype. The first galley proofs I ever saw contained her accounts of various concerts and minstrel shows in the Arctic Brotherhood Hall.

For most of my boyhood years she was also writing a novel. It was called "Then Alice Came Home" and it ran to several hundred pages. It was set in rural Ontario and England in the Nineteenth Century. She used to read sections of it aloud to us and I can still remember the first line: "Mrs. Barnes was making cookies." We all thought it was wonderful and were perfectly convinced that it would become a best seller and we would all be rich. Alas, it made the rounds of all the publishers but it never saw print.

My mother visited most of these publishers herself and listened carefully to what they told her and re-wrote her novel several times, always in vain. Several publishers were surprised that a woman living in the fabled Klondike would not write about the life around her. "Why don't you write about what you *know*?" they would ask. But my mother's attitude was that there was not much to write about in Dawson City. It did not occur to her then that she was living in a remarkable place at a remarkable period in history, that there was drama and adventure all around her, and that people were eager to read about it. She preferred to wrestle with the story of a titled Englishman working on an Ontario farm.

None of us, of course, saw anything remarkable in our environment. I saw nothing remarkable in my own parents and it was many years before I realized what very special people they were. It crept up on me, bit by bit and it continues to creep up on me. In the summer of 1971, I climbed the Chilkoot Pass for the first time with one of my daughters and one of my sons and it gave me an eerie feeling to realize that my father had come this way, seventy-three years before, and that *he* had packed on his back a year's supply of goods—food, clothing, equipment, tools, *everything*. That would have amounted to a good ton, which meant that he climbed the pass not once but dozens of times, carrying about sixty-five pounds each trip (we carried about twenty) and scaling that appalling, boulder-strewn incline day after day for the best part of a winter before building a raft and drifting through rapid and canyon to the gold fields, five hundred miles to the north west.

All this took stamina and guts and a sense of adventure of a kind that is not often found today. As a growing boy I tended to think of my parents as rather conservative fuddy duddies. Actually they were both gamblers. One has to remember the sheltered life that Edwardian ladies suffered to comprehend the enormity of my mother's decision to quit Toronto for a life in the northern wilds and then to marry a man with no prospects at all and to spend the first months with no other shelter than a tent and none of the accoutrements of civilization! Yet I scarcely ever heard my parents refer to those early years. My father was more interested in collecting wildflowers and looking at the stars and building a boat so that we might spend our summers on the river. My mother was working on her novel about farm life and the English aristocracy.

It was not until the mid-forties, many years after the events described here took place, that she began to get some perspective on the past. It was then that she started to work on the present manuscript. By that time, I, too, had begun to understand what a remarkable life both my parents had led.

In the early fifties, some years after my father died, she asked me to help her with a new draft of the book. My task was to make her understand that many of the things that had happened to her—and which she had originally omitted from the tale—were not nearly as prosaic as she believed. The result was the present book, which was completed in 1954, nine years after my father's death and twenty-two years after our family left the Yukon behind.

Since then it has become a minor Canadian classic, read by thousands, first as an intensely human adventure story and, second, as a piece of social history. It has been anthologized, serialized, translated and excerpted for the schools and in her twilight years it brought to my mother a modicum of fame, which she thoroughly enjoyed. Nothing pleased her more than to receive letters from men and women who had been moved by her story, or to be interviewed on television or radio, as she often was, or to be invited out and lionized. She was seventy-seven years old when the book was published and she lived to write another—a boy's novel about the Yukon this time. And in her eighty-ninth year, which was her last, she was still writing away, in spite of fading eyesight and a failing mind.

And so my memory of her in those last days is remarkably

similar to my earliest recollections: the deceptively frail figure hunched over the typewriter, pecking away and scratching out the result and writing it over again and again, as her father did before her and as her son has done after her. Books, after all, are the only monuments any writer desires. This is a good one, and as lasting, I think, as any granite.

PIERRE BERTON

Kleinburg, Ontario
January, 1972

Preface

THIS is a brave book. It is a record of a woman's courage and devotion in a hostile land. It is the story of a refined and sensitive girl who found happiness the hard way, and triumphed over conditions that would have driven most women to distraction. It is also a tribute to a husband who with hand, heart and head was outstanding in a world of worthy men.

I have read many books on the Yukon, but this is different. The simple narrative needs no frills, for back of it is a wealth of experience that would fill volumes. One feels that here is a paystreak rich and deep, and that the difficulty is not what to say but what to select. Yet though it is a first book there are luminous passages that a professional might envy.

Dawson in its hey-day has inspired many a pen, but here is Dawson in its decadence, a poignant picture truthful in detail. Like the author I cannot bear to think of it as a ghost town, and those who loved it will never see it that way. But we do not want to go back—that would hurt too much.

However, it is not this slant of the book that impresses me most. It is the gallant personality of the author, which shines on every page, and makes her chronicle a saga of the High North. There is so much she does not say, but lets us see between the lines—hardships and hazards, stress and struggle, the creation of a happy home with love and cheer. All this, told with humour, with graphic detail, and with a charm of style, makes the book a valiant one and one to be read with sympathy.

In the evening of life it is a ray of sunshine to have achieved success in a strange field, and I hope the author will reap a rich harvest. It is nigh half a century since I escorted her to a Dawson dance. . . .

> Dear lady, I will not forget,
> Though fifty years ago,
> Your maiden tresses black as jet
>   —Now white as snow.

ROBERT SERVICE

Foreword

THE seeds from which this book sprung were planted long ago, when I first began to write dispatches back from Dawson to the Toronto *Globe* and to *Saturday Night* in the years before the First World War. My father was a journalist and I was brought up in a writing climate. In a haphazard way, I have been writing all my life. But this book did not begin to germinate until my son, Pierre Berton, went back to the Klondike, which he had not seen for many years, to write some articles for *Maclean's Magazine*, of which he is an editor. For me, and for many other Yukoners, there was nostalgia in the things he wrote, for it was clear that Dawson had not changed greatly from the ghost town that I remembered a generation before. It was Arthur Coldrick, an old Yukon friend, whom the reader will meet occasionally in these pages, who started me thinking about a book on Dawson City. After reading the article, he wrote me:

> Pierre's piece on his home town delighted me. He didn't waste his time when he made his trip last summer. What a mass of material that land holds for the imaginative writer! I wonder you are not tempted to put some of your experiences in the form of a book. There is so much more than the dominance of masterful men, the behaviour of the common man and woman suddenly coming into the possession of riches, the unequal struggle of the unfit, and the sordid life of the vicious. . . .

These words set me thinking, and I began to set down, hesitantly at first, then more eagerly, my own memories of my days in the North and the fantastic collection of people

I knew there. In this task, I have had the professional assistance of my son, whose memories of the Klondike are as clear and sharp as my own. I should also like to thank the many Yukon pioneers who refreshed my recollections with facts and figures, people and places that I had half forgotten but felt deserved inclusion in this book. These include Mrs. I. O. Stringer, John A. Spence, Capt. M. Campbell of the steamer *Casca*, Charles J. Vifquain, A. E. Lee, Claude Bermingham, and Sergt. and Mrs. Stangrom of the R.C.M.P. The reader will meet some of them in the pages that follow.

To the best of my knowledge, everything in this book is true. The events occurred just as I have recorded them here. Occasionally, to avoid embarrassment, I have had to change a name or two, but I have not done this except where I felt it absolutely necessary.

Everybody, it has been said, has at least one book locked up inside them. Here is mine.

LAURA BEATRICE BERTON.

Vancouver, B.C.

One

I IMAGINE that in everyone's life there eventually comes a moment when a simple question, or a chance meeting, or a knock on the door, changes the entire course of one's future. My own moment came early on a hot summer's morning in 1907 with the ringing of the telephone while I was still shaking the sleep from my mind in the brass-knobbed bed in our home on Indian Road in Toronto.

The voice on the phone belonged to a Miss Currie, who was superintendent of Toronto kindergartens, and it was her prim tones on the other end of the line that changed my future.

"I've just received a wire from the superintendent of education for the Yukon. He wants me to send up a kindergarten directress for the school in Dawson City—someone who can sing and play the piano. Could you go, Miss Thompson?"

Miss Currie added hastily that it was a fine modern school, that she felt it a good opportunity, that she would have to know quickly and that the salary was $2100 a year. She might have omitted the first three items. The Toronto school board was paying me an annual $480. Without a moment's hesitation I answered yes. Men had risked death to rush to the Klondike for riches. Why not a twenty-nine-year-old kindergarten teacher?

All that I had heard of the Yukon and the Klondike to that point could have been inscribed on one page of a school copybook. Most of my information came from the reports of Faith Fenton, Klondike correspondent of the Toronto *Globe*. I had a confused impression of bitterly cold weather, dance-hall girls in big hats and gay dresses, grizzled miners in smoky saloons and men climbing ceaselessly up a snowy pass. I remembered the big Toronto shop windows of a few years before which had showed stalwart dummies in khaki miners' outfits working with pick and shovel, and the pans of gold nuggets on display. But I hardly knew where the Klondike was.

My father, a high-domed man with a great black beard, could only stare at me as if I had taken leave of my sanity. "You—in a rough mining camp?" he cried. "The whole scheme is absurd, child." He was a free-lance journalist by profession, a Quaker by breeding and a socialist by politics. He lived in a world of books and papers and long midnight discussions on abstract ideas. He was a nonconformist in almost every sense, but this evidence of a certain nonconformism on my part distressed and confused him. My religious sister, Maude, who had been an Anglican nun and was now preparing to be a missionary, and my artistic sister, Florrie, who was just back from a year of painting in Paris, both flung up their hands in horror. "All I can say is, I'm *very* sorry," Florrie kept repeating over and over, shaking her head as she did so. "The Wild West would be bad enough. But the uncultured Klondike —unspeakable!" My closest friend and fellow teacher, Winnie Ross, was more practical. "Why not try it for a year and see how you like it?" she said. That in the end was my decision, and I began to spend the hot days of midsummer searching for long winter underwear and heavy woollen clothing, collecting information about the mining camp and receiving advice from well-wishers.

There was plenty of the latter: "Be sure and tell everyone on the coast boat that you're going to teach. . . ." "I understand the Alaska steamers are filled with questionable women. One can't be too careful. . . ." "My dear, I would *certainly* wear a wedding-ring. You'd find it a great protection."

The only dash of cold water on my plans (other than from my family) came from Mrs. Harry Ridley, an old acquaintance who had actually been in Dawson City, where her husband, a lawyer, had practised for several years.

"Why on earth are you going to Dawson?" she wanted to

know. "Why, my dear, it's *all over*. They're all leaving. There's nothing there now."

If this intelligence was dispiriting, her next remark was confusion. I had begun to tell her about my purchases of woollens, when she brushed me aside. "Have you got a good evening dress?" she asked me. The question astonished me, but she promptly produced a wardrobe full of Paris creations which she said she'd brought back from Dawson with her.

"That's the sort of thing you'll need up *there*!" she told me. Later I was to wish that I had followed her advice.

The evening before I left, my father, following his usual custom, read aloud selections from Shakespeare and then recited Walt Whitman's "Pioneers, O Pioneers", of which he was very fond and which we all felt neatly fitted the occasion. I took a long look around the familiar parlour, lined with rows of books and huge steel engravings, for I felt—rightly, as it turned out—that I would see very little of this room or of my family in the years to come.

Almost before I knew it I had reached Vancouver, and was aboard the S.S. *Princess Beatrice* heading north up the Pacific Coast towards Alaska.

I looked with apprehension at my fellow passengers the first morning at breakfast, then smiled to myself at the memory of the various warnings I had received. If there ever was a respectable, unglamorous array of men and women, it was this motley group of travellers hurrying north. In my immediate vicinity there were three schoolteachers, two nuns, three nurses, four clergymen and a wireless telegrapher. I could not know it then, but some of them were to be my closest companions for years and others were to be my closest friends for life.

The teachers were to be my fellow workers in the Dawson public school. There was John Henry, a gaunt, shy Irishman with awkward hands and feet, who was to be the new science master. He kept to himself, for the most part, sitting alone under the stairs on the hurricane-deck, fixing his eyes on us when he thought we weren't looking and hurriedly averting them whenever we turned about. We were colleagues for five years in the Dawson school and neighbours for another five after that, but when our ways finally parted I did not feel I knew him any better than I did at the end of that four-day voyage.

Then there was Miss Hamtorf, who was returning to Dawson after a summer's absence. She was of German extraction and she looked it—a fine-looking, blonde woman in a well-tailored grey tweed suit, older than I but with a great deal of style about her. I liked her at once, for she was interested in good books and in ideas and had some knowledge of art. We became close friends, and although—as I later discovered—she had a caustic and sarcastic tongue and was inclined to harbour some of the suspicions of an old maid, she had a dry humour which compensated for it all.

The third teacher was Miss Ruler, a younger woman than I, colourless as to looks, manner and clothing, narrow-minded in her ideas, and straight and unbending as her name. She was a product of rural Ontario and I would have thought her uneducated had it not been for her university degree, of which she was fond of speaking. On deck she generally appeared to be deep in a book, but Miss Hamtorf and I noticed she never came to the end of it and we at once dubbed her The Bookworm.

The three nurses were all bound for the Good Samaritan Hospital in Dawson. Miss Hamtorf and I summed up Miss Moodie, the matron, as conscientious but fun-loving, Miss Burkholder as very pretty but a bit flirtatious, and Miss Lawson, older than the other two, as an earnest optimist who had the letters WCTU stamped on her features.

The clergymen on board made up a fairly good cross section of the Church in the North, as I was to see it in the years that followed. There were the Rev. Mr. Turkington, the Presbyterian minister for Dawson, jolly, earnest and thirty-eightish, and the Rev. Mr. Adam, the Methodist minister for Dawson, bland and moon-faced. Both were replacing the incumbent minister of their respective parishes and both were, in their turn, shortly to be replaced by other ministers. The Protestant ministers in Dawson, as I was to discover, came and went like flocks of migrating geese in the fall. (The Roman Catholic priests, on the other hand, hung on for decades.) It was often said that the White Pass railway and steamship line existed entirely on fares sold to the ever-changing procession of ministers, nurses, teachers and mounted policemen.

The Anglican missionary on board was Mr. Routsley, a stout, squat man with a great walrus moustache and a throaty English voice, who had the feeling of the North about him. Before the voyage was over I had learned something of his story. He had arrived at Fort Simpson as a carpenter in 1887, but had soon become ordained and had gone as a missionary among the Indians to other settlements in the North—Fort Liard, Fort McPherson, Fort Simpson, Fort Norman and Fort Yukon. Like so many men who live lonely and inaccessible lives in the wilderness, his tale had a whisper of minor tragedy about it. He had a sweetheart in England who had promised to marry him and whom he had sent for when he moved to Fort McPherson on the Arctic Circle. She had come obediently, making the long, arduous trip by boat and train and steamer, only to find, on arrival, that she no longer knew the man she was engaged to. "Who is it?" she asked in dismay as she stood on the deck of the river steamer and looked down at the figure on the bank with his ragged beard, his unkempt clothes and his dirty pipe. And the answer came back that this was the man she had promised to marry. Marry him she did, for she would not go back on her word, and the two of them lived together in a strange, uneasy partnership for all of the years that I knew them. How often was I to see this tale repeated with minor variations on its theme.

The highest-ranking clergyman on board, and by far the most remarkable, was the Anglican bishop of the Yukon, Isaac O. Stringer. He had been in the North since his graduation from theological college in 1892, unceasingly padding on snowshoes and paddling in canoe across the two hundred thousand square miles of his great diocese, which took in all of the Yukon and part of the North-West Territories and extended from the fifty-fourth parallel far north of the Circle. He was a tall, big-chested man, straight as a church steeple, with a high, intelligent forehead, clear blue eyes, fair hair and a look of absolute serenity. He was a "he-man" in the best sense and he was to prove it many times in the years to come.

His wife was a pleasant, round-faced, buxom woman, with a manner best described as "homey". To look at her you would never dream that she had stirred as much as a hundred miles from the Ontario farm on which she was raised. It was quite difficult for me to realize that since 1896 she had been living on Herschel Island in the Arctic Ocean, a treeless, wasted pinpoint in the cold ice-choked sea. She was the first and only white woman to live there among the Eskimos to whom her husband ministered, and for eight years she had not seen one of her own kind. As we leaned over the rail and watched the ragged green coast of British Columbia slip by she told me fragments of her story: how she had borne two children on the island and named one of them after it; how with a dog-team and two sleighs she had taken her family across the roof of the world one cold June, sleeping on the bare ice in a water-proof robe with the babies buttoned together in a sleeping-bag; how a knife-wielding Eskimo had invaded her cabin with murder in his eye, only to be routed by the cold tones of her husband, who hardly looked up from his shaving; how she had visited the sick in their igloos, crawling through underground passages over squirming dogs and decaying whale-meat; how, for comfort, she had learned to play the tiny organ the Hudson's Bay Company gave her as a wedding present to while away the endless Arctic night.

Now she too was going to live in Dawson, the See-city of the new bishop's diocese. To her, alone of all of us, it was like returning to the bright lights of civilization.

As we talked, the boat slipped slowly northward through the dark waters of the Inside Passage, an island-sheltered waterway that is more like a canal. We were entering the awakening North, still in the pioneer stage, and there was a sense of life and urgency all about us. The air was heavy with the scent of halibut and herring, for this was fish-canning country, and occasionally we would come upon a tiny village on barnacled stilts rising above a glistening, pungent beach left naked by the tide.

They were blasting the town of Prince Rupert out of the coastal granite when we arrived. The air was filled with the sound of whirring saw-mills and exploding dynamite. Stumps were burning, trees falling. The earth was raw, black and soaking wet, and a rough plank sidewalk did duty for a main street. The virgin forest crowded in on the irregular row of tents, log cabins and clean-smelling unweathered shacks. But there was life here—a bank was already doing business in a tent. There was a feeling of excitement in the air. I felt elated. Here was the frontier, literally being pushed back.

Ketchikan on the Alaskan Panhandle was bustling, too, and the sense of excitement was increased by the salmon run then in progress. From a little footbridge across a rushing mountain stream we watched hundreds of the bleeding, gasping fish struggling to reach their spawning grounds, in much the same way, I reflected, that men had bled and gasped up this very coast a few years before in their struggle to reach the Klondike.

The Indian towns were a contrast to all this white man's bustle and movement. At old Fort Simpson, the Indian women crouched Buddha-like over queer, mysterious-looking piles of wares in the market-place; the Indian girls with their fine skin and black eyes and kerchiefed heads strolled lazily along the main street; the Indian men lolled on the corners; the Indian babies with their tiny button eyes peeped curiously in neat clusters from behind the picket fences.

Skagway, when we reached it at the end of the sea journey, was a disappointment. Portal of Romance, the tourist folder had called it, and it certainly had a romantic setting, crouched at the base of the snow-covered White Pass mountains at the

head of the Lynn canal, a long, natural arm of placid green
water. But the town itself was black and dreary, the roads
rutted, the wooden sidewalks rickety, the buildings slowly
being torn down, the empty spaces filled with piles of rubble,
the shops and stores blank and boarded up. To this expiring
city twenty thousand men or more had made their pilgrimage,
flung up their hasty shacks, and just as hastily pushed on
north, leaving a handful of ragged, whiskered miners, who now
roamed the streets in coloured shirts and parkas.

Down the gangplank and into this ghost town we came in
our white shirt-waists and long tailored skirts, with our sailor
hats perched primly on our high pompadours. A neat gentle-
manly man named Hamilton rushed up to help me with my
bags. We had become friendly on the boat and the others had
scented a romance in the offing, but actually we had been
discussing socialism, a subject that would have astonished my
colleagues. Mr. Hamilton was a telegrapher on the Yukon
River—a quiet, studious man of about thirty who wore a
brown tweed cap and never smoked but always carried a copy
of Mary Baker Eddy's *Science and Health with Key to the
Scriptures* about with him. He said her faith had been "a
wonderful help" to him, but didn't specify how. He was highly
thought of by Miss Lawson, the elderly nurse with the WCTU
leanings. "Not at all like the wild young men one hears about
in the North," she kept saying. Now, as we walked down the
long wharf on the way to lunch at the Golden North Hotel, he
asked if he might show me the Whitehorse Rapids when we
arrived at the head of the Yukon River the following day. I
accepted, though I had been brought up never to accept dates
with young men with whose backgrounds one wasn't fully
familiar.

Shortly after this we boarded a little narrow-gauged train
and began to zigzag slowly up the twenty-nine hundred feet of
the famous White Pass over which so many gold seekers had
gone on foot a few years before. Beside the track there ran a
thin little path, still visible, worn by the plodding feet of

thousands of pioneers. Below us was the dizzy drop of Dead Horse Gulch, where three thousand pack-animals had perished in the summer of 1897. As we climbed high into the mountains and the snows, with three engines pulling us and another pushing from behind, it was easy to understand why this strange little railway, built at frightful expense, had been fully paid for through freight charges long before it was completed.

"Look, girls!" said Miss Burkholder, the pretty nurse, as we reached the international border on the summit. "There's a Mountie!"

The Mountie saluted gravely, grinned, then passed out of sight.

"Cheer up," said Miss Hamtorf drily. "There's a whole barracks full in Dawson."

Shortly after, we pulled into the station at Bennett, on the green glacial lake of the same name. The town of Bennett, where the stampeders had built the crude boats that took them down the Yukon River, could be seen across the water. "That used to be a very lively place indeed," Bishop Stringer remarked as we alighted. "Now there are scarcely a dozen people there. I suppose you'd call it a ghost town." As he spoke, the oncoming train from Whitehorse, bound for Skagway, puffed in to the platform. It was crammed with men, most of them bent on leaving the North for good. All seemed very jovial and most were a little drunk. Everybody seemed to know everybody else and there was a great deal of laughter and back-slapping all around.

A short man in a wide-brimmed black hat and a string tie, whom I later learned was W. W. B. MacInnes, the retiring commissioner of the Yukon, strode up to our group.

"What are you doing coming back?" he asked Miss Hamtorf. "It's dead, Miss Hamtorf! It's dead!"

"I'm crazy to be going back. I don't know why I'm doing it," said Miss Hamtorf, wanly.

"Well, there's no one left in Dawson," the ex-commissioner said. "Everybody's leaving. I mean *everybody*."

I felt a wave of dismay. This is what Mrs. Ridley, the lawyer's wife, had told me in Toronto before I left.

We lunched in the Bennett station in a great barn-like hall at long tables groaning with food. We ate braised moosemeat, macaroni and cheese, hash, baked beans, pickled beets, blueberry pie and canned milk. We had half an hour in which to eat, and the meal cost a dollar, which seemed very high to me, for you could eat table-d'hôte in a Toronto restaurant for fifty cents. In the next quarter century I was to eat many more meals in the White Pass Dining Room at Lake Bennett, and in all that time I cannot remember that the menu ever varied in a single detail. Twenty-five years later, the braised moosemeat, macaroni, beans and pie were identical with those I had on my first trip. And the price was still a dollar.

The train jogged on, past the thin finger of Lake Bennett ringed by a circle of mile-high peaks reflected in its mirror surface, through stubby forests carpeted with crimson fire weed, past lakes, rivers, canyons and rapids, until in late afternoon we reached Whitehorse, in the wide valley at the head of navigation on the headwaters of the Yukon. Again the platform swarmed with people, mostly men, all wanting to be introduced. Among the men were sprinkled a few fashionably dressed women, a policeman or two in scarlet and dozens upon dozens of husky dogs. Those ubiquitous dogs! I was seldom to be out of sight or sound of them for twenty-five years.

We put up at the White Pass Hotel, across from the railway-station. We entered a large lobby, dominated by an enormous sheet-iron stove, and ringed with chairs occupied by dejected-looking men, who eyed us with interest. Between each pair of chairs and slightly to the front stood an enamel spittoon. We registered in an enormous book and Miss Hamtorf and I decided to share a room, which also, it developed, meant sharing a bed. No room had a bath. No room had a key. Indeed, I seldom saw a key in the Yukon. Hotel rooms, stores, private houses all stayed open; thanks to the redcoats there was little crime.

That night we had a gay dinner in the hotel dining-room. The menu was almost identical with lunch—moosemeat, fresh blueberry pie, pork and beans. The price was still a dollar. "Table-d'hôte or à la carte?" I asked seriously when the waitress presented the menu. The entire room rocked with laughter. "Starter?" the waitress asked. "No, thanks," I said, thinking it some new kind of fish. It was apparent that I didn't yet speak the language.

Strangers kept coming over to our table to be introduced. Everybody seemed to know who we were, our full names, our destination, birthplace, occupation and background. This startled me, but I soon learned that a mysterious moccasin telegraph ran through the country. I could never explain it, though I always suspected that the telegraph operators themselves had something to do with it, for they were lonely men with little to do most of the time except to gossip on the wires. But it was a fact that there were few secrets in the Yukon. Once in Dawson a local wag coupled the name of a respectable Dawson woman with those of some leading prostitutes in chalk on a wall. The intelligence reached Whitehorse, four hundred miles away, within an hour, long before the defamed woman herself knew about it. A man from the Yukon could meet another man from the Yukon in Rome, Italy, and make some remark and within days, it seemed, that remark would be relayed north. A few days after I reached Dawson I sent a report of my trip back to the Toronto *Globe* and tried to preserve anonymity by using a pseudonym. It was useless. Before I had seen my own report in the paper my phone was ringing and people were commenting on it.

As we ate dinner a waiter came in with a tray of what he called "ice-worm cocktails", to the intense annoyance of the teetotalling Miss Lawson. Sure enough, the white worms, which we were told were considered a prime delicacy, could be seen at the bottom of each glass. They turned out, of course, to be spaghetti. This hoary joke was still being used on tourists and newcomers when I quit the Yukon for good.

Robert Service, whose *Songs of a Sourdough* had begun to excite interest outside, was a clerk in the local Bank of Commerce and we asked several people about him. Nobody seemed greatly impressed by his initial success and, although his books were on sale in the stationer's, few Whitehorse people had bothered to read them. Miss Hamtorf and I made two breathless journeys to the bank to see him, but on neither occasion was he there.

I hadn't seen Mr. Hamilton, the telegrapher who was to escort me to the Whitehorse Rapids, since Skagway, so it came as something of a shock the next morning when Miss Hamtorf said triumphantly at breakfast: "*Well!* I hear your friend has been on a tear. They say he has them regularly. You'd better come with us to the rapids."

"Don't believe all you hear," said Miss Lawson. "Perhaps he was tempted by evil companions. I'd go with him anyway. You're a good influence on him. I'm sure you could do a lot for that man if you wanted to."

I was filled with misgivings, but in a moment or two Mr. Hamilton himself arrived, somewhat defiantly. He was fairly sober but his face was pale, his eyes bloodshot, and his hands shaking. "I've been drinking," he said morosely, by way of opening the conversation. I had never seen a man in this condition before, though we had never been a teetotalling family and my father had occasionally arrived home late with his voice thicker than usual. What was to have been a pleasant outing now became an ordeal. Mr. Hamilton spent half his time apologizing for his condition and the other half quoting from the theories of Mary Baker Eddy, which he said were saving him, not too successfully it appeared, from drink. In addition the mosquitoes were eating me alive. I was in no mood to save Mr. Hamilton and it was with vast relief that, after the merest glance at the rapids, I got back to the hotel.

We left Whitehorse that evening on the steamer *Casca*, a white, three-storeyed river boat with gingerbread fretwork around the cabins, a yellow smokestack, and a bright red paddle-wheel at the stern. Behind us, the little town straggled along the flat, half-hidden in greenery, its front street a queer medley of log cabins, false-fronted stores and frame government offices. A boneyard of disused steamers marked the outskirts. Indians and Malemute dogs roamed the banks.

Next day it was evident that Mr. Hamilton was still drinking. I was in my cabin when Miss Lawson knocked and said she wanted my help. She had, she said, just seen the "poor young man" leave a bottle in his state-room.

"Now listen," she said, dropping her voice to a whisper. *"He must never have that bottle!* Do you understand me?"

I understood her only too well, and before I knew it she was leading me on tiptoe out the door, into the main dining-saloon and into his unlocked room. We found the bottle under his pillow and Miss Lawson tucked it under her coat. She clung to it firmly until we were back to safety, then tossed it triumphantly into the hissing waters of the river.

We did not see Mr. Hamilton again until ten that evening, when the steamer approached Cassiar Bar, where he was to disembark. Evidently we had not done our job well enough. We watched as the purser went to his room and steered his thoroughly inebriated passenger to the deck. The river was too low to dock at the bank so our friend was put off in a small boat. We watched him being rowed to shore in the dim light. We could just make out the outlines of two cabins, from one of which came a faint glimmer. Somewhere from behind the dark spruces came the yapping of Malemutes. It was a lonely-looking place for a drunken man to be left, and his plight was underlined when he saw us on the deck and stood up to wave an unsteady good-bye. He was unequal to it and fell flat on his face in the bottom of the boat.

" 'Here endeth the first lesson'," said Miss Hamtorf in her dry way. "A fitting introduction to the Yukon."

The steamer slipped easily downriver, stopping occasionally to take on cord-wood, which she burned voraciously, or to drop a passenger or two off into the wilderness. The eternal slap of the paddle-wheel and the periodic rumble of cord-wood being unloaded into the furnace well from hand-carts below decks disturbed our dreams or lulled our slumber depending on our temperaments. The whole land was aflame with autumn colours, the birches and aspens yellow, the shrubs above the timber-line crimson, the sky frost blue. Etched against it were ragged V's of mallard ducks going south for the winter like the people we had passed on the train.

The river itself, unrolling past us like an endless scroll, was eternally fascinating, for it boiled continually like a tea-kettle, breaking into continual eddies and whirlpools which hissed and gurgled as we went by. The water was low and the paddle-wheel churned it into a torrent which rushed up the sides of the steep bank for several feet as we slipped by. The watercourse itself twisted continually—there wasn't a quarter mile of straight stretch on the entire trip—and although the general course was north, we were often travelling west or east. In fact, at one place opposite Eagle Mountain, called Taylor's Cut-Off, we made such an abrupt hairpin turn that for a distance of seven miles the steamer's compass veered the entire hundred and eighty degrees.

At the entrance to this wooded peninsula the steamer gave an abrupt whistle and pulled up to shore and we were told that anyone who wished to might follow a path across the neck of land and wait for the boat to pick them up on the opposite side. Led by Mr. Turkington, the Presbyterian minister, we set off through the thickets of berries and bright autumn leaves to the other side of the peninsula, where we rejoined the steamer three hours later.

The river from this point on was networked with channels and sloughs, some narrow and shallow, others as wide and as fast as the main body. They had told us in Whitehorse that the trip to Dawson would take forty hours, "unless"—a word that covered all sorts of uncontrollable situations and explained why the steamers kept to no rigid schedules. But we were in no hurry, and when the boat stuck fast on a sand-bar at a spot appropriately named Hell's Gate we greeted the mishap cheerfully. Only one incident marred this sojourn for me. We were close to an Indian encampment and many of the passengers wanted to photograph the natives. They were a shy, primitive people wearing large rings through their noses, and they fled in terror when they saw the cameras. Nothing daunted, the photo fiends persisted, charging the fleeing Indians from every quarter without success. It was at this stage that Mr. Routsley, the walrus-moustached missionary, stepped in. "Wait a bit— I'll get 'em for you," he cried, and seized two squirming women, whipped them about and held them to be photographed, laughing jovially all the time. I never warmed to Mr. Routsley after that and began to comprehend something of the feelings of the woman who had gone out to him in the wilderness and found him a stranger.

We were aground two days on the sand-bar, then moved off again down the lonely river, with its lonely little cabins and its lonely men. Somewhere round the bend was the golden city of Dawson. There was a sharp autumn chill in the air and I felt buoyant with anticipation. I had received my northern baptism, eaten my first moosemeat, encountered my first drunk, met my first sourdough. Romance in many forms lay quite literally just round the corner.

Two

DAWSON lay sprawled out before us, a crowded collection of grey buildings huddled close together on a strip of beach and swamp at the base of a tapered mountain. Seen from the steamer's deck, the buildings seemed an odd assortment. There were large, square government buildings, innumerable long, low warehouses, irregular rows of frame stores with rickety false fronts, two-storeyed log hotels, banks, saloons, dance-halls, and tucked in everywhere—squeezed between shops, oozing out of alleys, squatting on the water's edge, overflowing on the hillside, clinging to rocky cliffs, sprawling on the opposite shore—were hundreds of small log cabins and tiny shacks not unlike enlarged dog kennels.

The effect was indescribably drab, for all the large buildings were painted grey and all the roofs were zinc and all the trees had been cut down by the stampeders. The town was dominated by a great shell-shaped scar on the mountain, a slide which the legends said had buried an Indian village a century before.

Already the steamer had passed the foaming mouth of the Klondike River. Now it was swinging into the high dock, and here I had my first glimpse of the people who were to be my neighbours for most of my life.

I don't think I had ever seen so many men before. The dock was packed with them: tall, ruddy-faced, broad-shouldered men mostly, all of them young or in their early prime, and in every conceivable kind of costume. There were miners in mukluks and mackinaws, jumpers and parkas, surveyors in neat khaki togs, Englishmen in riding-breeches, police officers in immaculate blue and gold, police constables in the familiar Mountie scarlet, and on the edge of the throng clusters of Indians in beaded skin coats and moccasins. There were perhaps only a dozen women on the dock. If the town itself was drab, this scene was alive with colour. If Dawson was dead, I asked myself, what must it have been like when it was alive?

Down the gang-plank we came, carrying our suitcases and boxes, the cynosure of all eyes and, it is safe to say, the chief topic of conversation at every dinner table that night. The superintendent of education, T. G. Bragg, a suave, neat widower with blue eyes and a blond moustache, welcomed us and conducted the three of us teachers through the town to a boarding-house which would provide us with temporary quarters. Our progress along the high, wooden sidewalks was slow, for the streets were busy, and Mr. Bragg seemed to be introducing us to the entire population.

As we passed a fruit store opposite the dock, a homely little man with a thatch of black hair and a pock-marked face rushed out at us with an outstretched hand and a wide grin of welcome. He was introduced to us simply as "Apple Jimmy", a name which I later learned he had got in '98, when he sold apples at a dollar apiece. Jimmy Oglow was quite obviously a town fixture. For almost fifty years, until his death, he was a self-appointed welcoming committee for all tourists, and an irresistible salesman of oranges and apples at three dollars a dozen. For a fabulous sum he could sell you a deep box of fruit, the top layer perfect specimens, and all beneath rotten, with a smile of angelic sweetness and a gracious phrase of broken English.

Then there were men in rough overalls who came up to say "how do" and who we thought were labourers, but who turned out later to be leading citizens. The women who stopped to chat were equally astonishing. They were dressed in the highest of fashion and their style and deportment would have done credit to Toronto or Montreal.

As we ambled along I had a confused kaleidoscopic

impression of black mud roads, deeply rutted and edged with great ditches, of vast numbers of large and beautiful dogs, of the black skeletons of frozen plants in the window-boxes, of huge pansies smiling hardily through frosted flower-beds, of French evening gowns in luxurious arrays in the dress shops and of meat at fifty cents a pound in the butcher shops— exactly double the Toronto price.

And so we arrived at "Kenwood", Miss Kenny's log boarding-house on Third Avenue, a gaunt, two-storey building standing stark and unadorned flush with the wooden sidewalk. Miss Kenny turned out to be a lively pioneer woman, pretty and petite, with rosy cheeks, sharp black eyes and an active tongue.

The door opened into a large living-room dominated by a huge sheet-iron Yukon furnace going full blast. By way of greeting I complimented Miss Kenny on its terrific heat. "Bah!" cried Miss Kenny. "Them sourdoughs, they make me tired bragging to the tourists about the cold!" She began to mimic the sourdoughs, "Oh, yes, ma'am, I often sleep in sixty-below weather . . . never feel the cold in the Yukon, ma'am, just roll my blanket in the snow, warm as toast." Miss Kenny put her hands on her hips in a characteristic attitude. "And next morning down they come whining for dear life: 'Miss Kenny, can't you give me more heat? My room is freezin'.' Ah-h—sourdoughs!"

That night, in my bedroom, I had my first experience with Dawson's "telephone walls". In almost every Dawson dwelling, the interior walls were simply made of cotton stretched on thin, rough boards, with wallpaper pasted over it. There was no plaster anywhere in the North. Through these paper-thin divisions every whisper was transmitted, and Miss Kenny's boarding-house, like most buildings in town, was nothing more than a great partitioned tent. All night long my slumber was haunted by the heartracking sobs of a young mining engineer, whose wife had died in a log cabin on the creeks. Sometimes in my dreams today his sobs come back to rack me across the decades. His mother was with him through the night and I can still hear her serene and beautifully modulated voice reading the verses of "The Light of Asia" to him against the harsh counterpoint of his sorrow. His name was Guy Lewington and he later became one of my closest friends. He was an engineer with the North American Trading and Transportation Company, nervous and high-strung but with great charm and delightful manners. He was English and because of his accent he was, I think, always considered a little strange by the Dawson people.

Miss Kenny kept a good table. She had a Japanese cook, as many Dawson people had, but the thing that surprised me was the quantity and quality of the fresh vegetables at every meal. Their size and their quite remarkable flavour was explained by the long, hot summer days (it was never dark) and the fact that the ground is frozen two feet from the surface. As a result, the lettuce and celery were far superior to anything I had tasted before.

Miss Kenny's clientele consisted of transients and permanent guests in about equal numbers. There was an American from the lower river who told us tales of the Nome Stampede; two miners, partners, in from the Sixty-mile country, who were collecting a grub-stake for a reported strike up the White River; and a great many Alaskans on their way upriver to Whitehorse and the Outside. My table mates consisted, besides the teachers, of two stenographers and two other couples, a postal clerk and a customs clerk and their wives. It is interesting to look back on these first acquaintances in Dawson and reflect on their various fates: one of the stenographers got married to a prominent lawyer and left town; the other, a short time later, left Dawson suddenly for Eagle, Alaska, where she tried to bring on an abortion and died of haemorrhage and infection. Mr. Wilson, the postal clerk, was drowned when he went through Five Finger Rapids in a canoe; his widow lived out the rest of her years in Whitehorse. Mr. Betts, the customs man, was a good tenor who sang sentimental songs at Dawson concerts and was a pillar of the Church of England choir. He was singing in the choir that first Sunday when I attended church, and twenty-five years later, on my last Sunday in Dawson, he was singing still. Thus, in various ways, did the country have its effect on the residents of Miss Kenny's boarding-house.

In addition to these, there was a fourth teacher, Miss Semple, who had preceded us to Dawson. She was a very pretty, quiet girl, attractive to and attracted by men. Miss Hamtorf always said, a little acidly, that Miss Semple had come in first to look over the ground and get a beau before we arrived. Whatever the truth of this, she certainly had a great many. She had black hair, a white complexion, a classical nose and great blue eyes. At parties she would sit quietly in one corner while the rest of us danced and laughed and played the piano and entertained. "Why, you've made the evening, Miss Thompson!" men would say to me gallantly. But next day the phone would ring continually for Miss Semple.

It was an unwritten rule that the four female teachers would live together, for the Victorian proprieties were such that no woman could live by herself in Dawson City and maintain her self-respect. There was no problem about finding a house to rent cheaply in Dawson. Meat and butter might be selling for double the accepted price, but homes were a drug on the market. From a population of thirty thousand plus in 1898, the town had dwindled to twelve thousand, and within a few years it would be down to about three thousand. We quickly got a five-room, two-storey log house on Seventh Avenue under the hill, fully furnished, for twenty-five dollars a month. We rented it from a lawyer, who, like almost everybody else it seemed, was leaving town on the last boat.

The four of us had little in common besides the fact that we followed the same profession. I was closer to Miss Hamtorf than to the others, for, though I occasionally found her caustic temperament trying, we liked the same kind of people, and she enjoyed a long walk, as I did. We had nicknames for the other two. Miss Semple we soon dubbed the The Belle, and Miss Ruler, of course, would always be The Bookworm. The latter turned out to be as colourless as I first thought her. She came from the Bible belt of Southern Ontario and was very strait-laced about religion. I remember one time when she was very worried about her mother, who was ill, and we were all sympathizing with her. One Sunday night, when the mail came in, I found a letter in her box from home and hurried to her with it. She refused to open it. "I don't read letters on Sunday, Miss Thompson," she said primly. "And after this please leave my mail in the box." Her sole interest, outside of books, was the popularity of her new-found friend, The Belle. The two shared a room together and went to the length of calling each other by their first names, an almost unheard-of familiarity. In the five years I knew Miss Hamtorf we never allowed ourselves this intimacy. We were always "Miss" to everyone and everyone was "Miss" to us.

Somehow, I found myself with the smallest room in our new home. It was also the coldest. When I lay on my narrow cot, my head jammed against one wall and my feet touched the frosted window on the other side. To keep out the sub-zero weather I tucked my new fur coat between me and the outside wall. In the morning I would often find it stuck hard in frost.

At first we hired a little Japanese cook, but he soon went back to the mining camps and was replaced a by stolid Swedish woman named Ida. She, too, left us to get married. Shortly after, Miss Hamtorf and I met her on the street and paused for a few words of greeting.

"Good-bye, Ida," I said in parting, for she, too, was leaving Dawson for ever. "I hope you'll be happy."

She glared. "Don't 'Ida' me," she said. "It's Mrs. Forrest now, see? I'm just as good as you and I got better clothes. You girls call me Ida and I'll call you Laura and Edith!"

My kindergarten opened a few days after our arrival. I was delighted with it. One thing that astonished me at first was the number of lights hanging from the ceiling. There were twelve on long cords. But when the sun left us for two months, early in December, and it was still twilight at noon, I soon saw their need. The windows, astonishingly, were filled with flowering plants. It turned out that the school janitor, Turner Townsend, was also the town florist. He used the schoolrooms to try to weather his crop over the dark winter season. They always started out magnificently, but as the sun left us they grew more and more straggly and anaemic until, by spring, they were hardly recognizable as plants at all, but looked more like strange white or grey-green fungi.

The children were the sons and daughters of pioneers, and I thought them unusually bright and responsive. None was backward in expressing himself, but few were bold or rude. They were northern born, all of them, and many were to stay in Dawson until their late twenties without ever seeing city lights or the traditional street-car. Their chatter was often amusing and, as with most children, it accurately reflected the attitudes and personalities of their parents. A few days after I opened the kindergarten, I listened to a heated argument on the question of women smoking.

"I tell you, ladies never smoke," the son of a Presbyterian elder was insisting.

"They do so," said a plump little girl whose mother was a prominent socialite.

"Sure they do," said a six-year-old whose family lived on the edge of Dawson's well-populated red-light district. "I see the ladies in Klondike City smoking all the time."

I soon discovered, with certain dismay, that little Johnny's or Mary's stories of what teacher said or did or wore each morning became topics of vital interest around the family dinner table each night. One morning during a marching exercise I promised that the best two soldiers would be allowed to carry the flag. The honour fell to two brothers named Smith. But to my astonishment, when I held out two small Union Jacks as the prize, I met with a rebuff. The boys stubbornly refused to have anything to do with them.

"Won't carry the flag," the elder Smith muttered.

"He's American," several children chorused. "He wants the Stars and Stripes."

I had not yet realized the extent of Dawson's American population, but this incident brought it home to me. All my arguments were useless. The little boys refused to capitulate and we moved on to a new game. By nightfall there were a dozen versions of this affair all over town. The Smith boys had "stamped on our flag" (Canadian version); the teacher had "forced them to wave the Union Jack" (American version). Next morning, the Smiths did not appear in kindergarten and a worried Mr. Bragg called me in. He told me I was perfectly right, that in his opinion the town had catered too much to resident Americans, but that he didn't want to stir up any fuss and in the future I was to ignore such incidents. Dawson was indeed, in some respects, an American island under Canadian rule. Up until the year I arrived, the Fourth of July had been the town's major celebration and Washington's Birthday was still being marked by a huge formal ball.

It was a cosmopolitan city. There were Americans from every state in the union, Canadians from every province, monocled Englishmen, Australians, Latin Americans, South Africans and Orientals. One of my first escorts was an Italian named Pagliacci, who taught me to make spaghetti. For some reason Chinese were barred from the country, but there was one half-caste and there were Japanese by the score. And there was a handsome, turbaned East Indian who used to mush into town from the creeks, standing erect behind a long team of huskies. I can still see him with the frost thick on his eyebrows, contrasting with the deep brown of his face.

"Jock" Spence, the town's leading grocer, told me some years later, in his thick Scots burr, that in order to cater to his customers' varying tastes he had to import luxuries from all over the globe. Freight rates were so high that it didn't pay to bring anything in but the best, and the stores were stocked with top-grade caviare, anchovies, lobster and shrimp. One winter,

Jack Donald, the general manager of the Northern Commercial Company, who was on a buying trip Outside, was rushed back to Dawson to solve a major crisis: they had run out of almonds, a terrible situation, for salted nuts were mandatory at every social gathering.

The shops reflected the cosmopolitan atmosphere. On Second Avenue there was a drab little store with a glittering interior, full of hand-made French evening dresses and operated by an old-country Frenchwoman named Madame Aubert, who went to Paris each year to bring back imported gowns and hats. Across the street, a little Japanese named Kawakami did a thriving business in silks, kimonos, parasols, linens, incense, porcelain, china and lacquer work. He was a curious little creature, entirely detached from the town. He received an enormous number of letters, and this caused many people to think he was a spy. But he was merely a seeker after truth, a quizzical little man with an enormous curiosity about the world. He sat beside his stove at the back of his shop, forever reading his *Encyclopaedia Britannica*. He had started with "aardvark" and was working methodically through it, year after year. In my final year in Dawson he had at last reached the Z's, but his features had, if anything, become more quizzical and his little eyes more bewildered. Then, having read everything, he died, his thirst for knowledge still unslaked.

The town, on closer inspection, was not the drab collection of tin-roofed shacks it had seemed to be from the steamboat's deck. It was not a beautiful city, but it certainly had character. It occupied a strip of beach and swampy ground a mile and a half long and half a mile wide. Its northern boundary was the Midnight Dome, a gently tapering wooded mountain of about eighteen hundred feet. Its southern boundary was the turbulent Klondike River. On its western flank lay the great Yukon; on its east, the low Klondike hills. Although these were the recognized city limits, the town actually spilled over, across both rivers and up the sides of the hills. Across the Klondike lay Klondike City, more commonly referred to as

Lousetown, for it housed the red-light district. Across the Yukon lay West Dawson, dominated by the ornate Villa de Leon, a miniature castle of white frame, built by two brothers whose wealth had been accumulated operating hotels in Dawson. Like so many other buildings it now stood empty and boarded up. Not far away were more ghostly symbols of Dawson's vanished glitter—the rows of rotting river boats in the White Pass Company's Boneyard. They stood keel to keel, their paint peeling, their great twin stacks rusting, the shrubbery growing high above their gangplanks.

On the hills above the city, to the east, lived a variety of curious men in tiny, immaculate log cabins with thick sod roofs. Miss Hamtorf and I used to go for walks up the old A.C. Trail (built by the Alaska Commercial Company) that led up the hill, and hear the sounds of gramophones filtering through the woods. There were Deephole Tomson, a gaunt man with long beard, and Donald Donald, a short little Scotsman known throughout the town as "Twa Donalds", and a miner named Caribou Cameron. There was also a French chef who used to make great bakings of French bread, and we could see the long loaves sitting on top of his mud roof where he had laid them out to freeze. It was necessary to keep the A.C. Trail open during the winter, because the town's main cemetery was on top of the hill. In winter the trail was a mass of glacier, for there were natural springs under it and the ice had to be chopped out and covered with sand every time there was a death in the town. One winter, one of the men on the hill left his cabin to go work a claim on the creeks. A spring under the cabin began to work and when he returned the entire house was jammed with solid ice which encased furniture, stove, utensils and tools in a giant cabin-sized block and held them in suspension. After the cabin was filled with ice it began to squeeze from the chimney, and those men who needed water would simply chop it off in sections, as it emerged.

Dawson City proper was laid out neatly on a checkerboard plan into streets and avenues, but there was no real feeling of neatness about the town-site, for the buildings all nudged each other crazily or spilled into the back lanes and narrow alleys. Many of the houses were built of the roughest kind of lumber, often old packing-cases. One had a front wall that consisted of the entire stern of a ship. There were huts made of stripped poles cemented by mud and clay, others composed wholly of tar-paper on a frame, and some made of petrol tins opened up and flattened out. The neat log cabin with its mud roof and its moss-chinked walls and its carefully notched and matched logs was the aristocrat. There was one next door to us owned by a clerk in the Northern Commercial Company and it was an incongruous sight in the early summer to see him in his dressing-gown on top of his roof at three o'clock in the morning in the bright sunlight, planting pansies and nasturtiums and schizanthus in the rich loam.

The major structures in Dawson belonged to the rococo school of frontier architecture familiar to students of Western films. It emphasized the false front, the bay window, the carved balustrade and the ornamental, scrolled fretwork. The dance-halls had almost reached the end of their days when I arrived in Dawson, but they were still operating that first winter and we teachers used to watch the girls, gaily and richly dressed, walking down to work about eight o'clock each evening. In the old days they had received a percentage of the drinks sold, and their main task had been to steer the customers to the bar, but this practice was slowly being stifled as the town grew in respectability. There were still several dance-halls going and there was a very large number of hotels, for Dawson was a transient's town. One night, Miss Hamtorf and I walked all over town and counted the saloons. There were twenty-eight of them. On this same trip we ran across another vestige of the old days, a man known simply as "The Spieler". Every evening he would stand on Front Street and in a stentorian voice, amplified by a megaphone, call out the events of the day. He was drunk most of the time, a stocky man with red hair and red, bleary eyes, but drunk or sober his voice could be heard over the entire city. In the old days, there had been one in front of every dance-hall, saloon and gambling-house, like barkers on a midway.

The hotels, like the saloons, were doing a roaring business and I was surprised at the number of them. The best, and one of the oldest, was the Regina, a three-storeyed white building with many turrets and a long, sloping, zinc roof, painted green. Another first-class hotel was the Fairview, which had a lively history. It had been built by a big Irishwoman named Belinda Mulroney, who had come into the Klondike with only fifty cents to her name, which she had flung dramatically into the river as she stepped off the boat. She started out on Bonanza Creek with a small hash-house, acquired interests in several valuable properties, and married a dapper champagne sales-man who called himself the Count de Carbonneau. It was as a countess that she left Dawson. The Fairview and Regina hotels were favourite places for evening dinner when I came to Dawson.

On Front Street in the old dance-halls, so they said, Chris Johansen, a tousled little miner from Whiskey Hill on Hunker Creek, had offered Cecile Marion, a plump, black-eyed dance-hall girl, her weight in gold if she'd marry him. They had weighed her out on a pair of huge scales and at a hundred and thirty-five pounds her price came to twenty-five thousand dollars. Here, too, Cad Wilson had taken her bath in wine and sported her famous fifty-thousand-dollar belt of matched nuggets. The famous Floradora dance-hall still stood on Front Street, run by Murray Eads and his wife, a former dance-hall singer. It stood in the exact centre of the most-storied block of all. The names of the "greats" of those gaudy days, a decade before, were still on everyone's lips: Babe Wallace, and Diamond Tooth Gertie and the Oregon Mare, so-called because she would whinny loudly across the dance-floor; Jack London, Wilson Mizner, Tex Rickard and Alexander Pantages; Nellie the Pig, who got her name from biting off a bartender's ear; Swiftwater Bill Gates, who bought up every egg in town at two dollars apiece to spite a girl friend; and Nigger Jim Daugherty, who started a mad stampede to nowhere on a bet.

The Floradora didn't last out the season, for the dance-hall era had reached its end. Murray Eads made some changes and the Floradora became the Royal Alexandra Hotel, and one of the town's leading hostelries. There was always some of the aura of the golden era about it. In the lobby hung three giant oil pictures of nudes, seven feet high, in tremendous gilt frames. Eads had had them packed in on men's backs over the trail in the early days. That hotel lobby, with its enamel spittoons, its painted nudes, its black-leather Edwardian chairs and its endless poker game glimpsed through the doors at the rear, never changed in any single detail in all the years I lived in Dawson.

But, already, decay was casting its chill breath across the town. Front Street was lively enough, but Second Avenue and Third Avenue, though they still contained many thriving shops, were on the verge of becoming a desert of second-hand shops and junk yards. Some of the buildings were already vacant and the windows boarded up. The second-hand shops were jammed with the refuse of the gold rush: stoves, furniture, gold-pans, sets of dishes, double-belled seltzer bottles, old fur coats, lamps, jardiniers, cooking utensils, rubber boots, hand organs, glassware, bric-à-brac, silver, and beds, beds, beds. Among the weeds of the vacant lots were piles of rusting mining machinery—boilers, winches, wheelbarrows and pumps. Behind the school stood two huge keystone drills, a storey in height, slowly rusting away. They were there when I arrived and they were there when I departed and I dare say they are still there. There was machinery all over the town and along the river bank. Some of it had been used and discarded, some had never been in use at all.

Up on the hillside you could see the thin line of the great Acland Ditch, an ambitious engineering project that, in the early days, had carried water for miles along the hills to the mining areas. It was an incongruous thing to come upon, during our walks through the woods, for it was a full six feet deep and three feet wide. It was dry now, and choked with weeds, the timbers of its flume, where it crossed the great slide, rotting away like the town itself.

As winter came on and navigation on the river ceased, the terms "outside" and "inside", "going out" and "coming in", which had first bewildered and amused me, began to take on a more significant meaning, and I found myself using them as unconsciously as my neighbours and to realize the aptness of the expressions. For we were now cut off from the outside world. The river was slowly being choked with the great cakes of ice that moved sluggishly past the town. Snow was falling thickly and the hills were already white. But it was too early for the six-horse stage-coach, the winter link with civilization, to begin its trek to Whitehorse, for the river could not yet be crossed. We were indeed imprisoned on the Inside, living with ghosts of an earlier decade.

Three

WITH the onslaught of winter I was plunged pell-mell into the ornate labyrinth of Dawson society. It was an eye-opener to discover that within this motley collection of log cabins and rickety frame dwellings, the most elaborate events proceeded without cessation in the grandest Edwardian style. In Dawson's golden days, when the town was full of newly minted million-aires, the city had been the Paris of the North in every sense. Now the glory and the glitter were beginning to fade, but the Dawson people were determined to keep up appearances, and keep them up they did all the years I lived there.

During my first week in Dawson I received my initiation into Dawson's social life at a reception at Government House by Mrs. Alex Henderson, the wife of the federal commissioner, or governor, of the Yukon. The actual Government House had burned down the previous year in one of the town's many fires, so while a new one was being constructed the Hendersons had taken up temporary quarters in a square two-storeyed home with wide verandahs on Ping Pong Alley, not far from the federal administrative buildings. It was to this building that Miss Hamtorf and I made our way at four o'clock in the after-noon. To my astonishment we found ourselves preceded by two distinguished-looking gentlemen in morning coats and silk hats which contrasted strangely with the surroundings.

Indeed, as soon as we were ushered inside by an immaculate Japanese servant in white, I felt again as if I might have been in Toronto or Montreal. Mrs. Henderson, a handsome, aristo-cratic-looking woman in her forties, was receiving in the wide doorway. Her dress of soft grey voile and lace contrasted sharply with the Indian and Eskimo relics on the wall. I laid my engraved card on a silver salver already piled high with other cards, and moved into the main room to mingle with the large crowd of fashionably dressed women and impeccably tailored men. The two big rooms were gay with pink-shaded lights and huge bouquets of asters, preserved carefully for this moment (I learned later) by Hawkins, the gardener, a man who looked as if he might have stepped straight from a Dickens novel. We took tea, poured into delicate porcelain cups from an elaborate silver service by the town's two leading socialites, Mrs. Z. T. Wood, wife of the police commissioner, and Mrs. James McAndrew, wife of a leading lawyer. I can still see these two women, seated regally at a lace-covered table dominated by tall candles· and bouquets; Mrs. Wood, erect and handsome (the Dawson people called her "stuck-up"), and Mrs. McAndrew, with a figure like a ripe peach, in a rose panne-velvet gown and a large hat that fairly dripped willow plumes. She was a lustrous woman and they called her "The Siren" behind her back.

Towards five o'clock, the Commissioner himself came in with a group of Government men. He was a round, balding man of great affability. One of his first acts on being appointed to the commissionship was to tighten the laws about the service of liquor in the dance-halls. As a result he effectively brought Dawson's dance-hall era to its close that winter, and before the season was out they had all closed their doors, never to reopen again, but to stand silently along the wooden sidewalks of Front Street with boarded-up windows and fading false fronts, as monuments to that gayer era when wine had flowed like bath-water and a woman could be weighed in gold dust.

Thus the party moved on, the cards piling higher in the salver, the tea flowing in an unending cascade, the fashionable women gliding through the crowd passing those refreshments which the local social rules decreed must be served at such gatherings: salted almonds, stuffed olives, home-made Turkish delight, fudge and maple creams, and pineapple sherbert. In all my years in Dawson, no party was complete without these basic essentials.

As we were about to leave, Miss Hamtorf introduced me to a pretty, saucy-faced woman with steel-blue eyes and an expression of unqualified determination. This was Mrs. George Black, the wife of a local lawyer and a leading member of the Conservative Party. I decided, as we chatted, that in spite of her mobile lips she would be a hard woman to cross, and when I later learned her story I knew I was right. She was an American from Chicago who had been deserted by her husband *en route* to the Klondike in 1898. None the less, she had pressed on up the coast of Alaska (sharing a three-tiered berth with a gambler and his mistress) and up the icy steps of the Chilkoot Pass. She had come down the river in a home-made boat, only to find herself pregnant shortly after her arrival in Dawson, by the husband who had left her. Too poor to buy hospital space, she had borne her child alone in a log cabin on the hill above Lousetown. She had raised money, bought a saw-mill, bossed sixteen men on a mining claim, divorced her husband and married George Black, who was to become one of the leading political figures in the North during the next half century. She was not yet too well known in town but she certainly made an impression on me.

"You'll be keeping a day, of course," she said breezily, in a voice that was more of a flat statement than a question, and without waiting for my reply, added firmly, "Well, be sure and let me know—I'll be there!"

The "day" she spoke of was part of the town's social fabric. Anybody who was anybody, and some who weren't, had a day. All my life in Dawson I had one on the second Tuesday of the month. On one's day, one was at home to the entire town during the hours of the late afternoon and early evening. One spent many days before *the* day salting the almonds, preparing the olives, churning the sherbert in the freezer, preparing trays of home-made candies. One made sure the proper people were honoured by being allowed to "pour" or "pass", and the coefficient of success was calculated in direct ratio to the number of people who turned up. Thus it was possible to compute the social standing of the entire upper crust of Dawson City mathematically.

As a result of this convention it was possible—nay, necessary —to attend an At Home every week-day afternoon. Sometimes, on crisp winter days when we had been in the stuffy schoolroom all day, Miss Hamtorf and I would rebel at the idea of attending another day. "Isn't it ridiculous," we used to tell each other. "How much nicer it would be to go for a long walk." But in the end we went to tea, to see and to be seen, for it was a great social snub to the hostess not to attend.

We teachers held our own day early in October, and we were able to count forty guests, including Mrs. Henderson, the commissioner's wife—really quite a creditable turnout, we told ourselves. (Each of the forty calls, of course, had to be returned.) Mrs. Stringer poured and, true to her promise, Mrs. Black attended. There was always a certain flamboyancy about her which I enjoyed. I remember, at that first At Home, asking her what she would take. She paused for an instant and then, raising one hand, called out in a firm, dramatic voice, "*Two* olives!" And that is all she had.

"What grit she's got, that woman," Miss Hamtorf said to me, not without admiration, when our day was ended. "They say the whole society crowd snubbed her at first after she married George Black. That didn't faze her a bit. She simply gave a big tea herself—sent cards to everyone whether they'd called on her or not—and although the Big Bugs vowed they'd never go, they all went in the end and it was a big success. Now she's invited everywhere."

The town, I soon discovered, was full of Blacks. Besides Mrs. Black and her husband George, there were his younger brother Charlie Black, another lawyer, and his uncle John Black, a third lawyer. All were from New Brunswick and all were staunch Conservatives and therefore opponents of the governing regime, which was Liberal. In future years people were to remark, with great truth, that there were only two political parties in the Yukon: the Liberals and the Blacks.

John Black and I quickly became great friends and remained so. He was a patriarchal man with a pointed white beard and a courtly manner, always immaculately turned out in morning clothes and always a stickler for etiquette. Conservatism was his creed and John A. Macdonald, the founder of the party, was his god. Everybody in town called him by his initials, J. B. He had a tenor voice, and on my first Sunday in church he caught my eye from his position in the choir and soon had me a choir member. He was, like so many others in that strange little ghost of a city, a lonely man. His story paralleled so many others in Dawson. His wife had come up one summer to visit him, but that one summer in the North had been enough for her and she had returned again to her own idea of civilization. Yet he remained for more than two decades, faithful to the Yukon, living alone in his neat little cabin.

Although, in theory, anyone in town could turn up at one's At Home, in practice only the socially acceptable attended. The social level began, of course, with the commissioner and his wife, and worked its way down through the judges and officers of the police, the high civil servants, the heads of the large companies, the bishops and church people, the bankers and bank clerks, lawyers and nurses until it stopped with us teachers, who clung to the charmed group by our finger-nails. It surprised and pleased me to find that teachers were regarded as socially acceptable in Dawson City, for in Toronto the profession was certainly no stepping-stone to social eminence. The Mounted Police, noncoms and constables, were not admitted to Dawson's social set—not even Sergeant Joy, a dapper Englishman with a waxed moustache and a public school education. Below the first social level came the merchants, who were known as "the downtown crowd", and below them the labourers, policemen and so on, who were, in turn, several steps above the dance-hall girls and the prostitutes of Klondike City and the half-breeds and Indians.

There were, in addition, a number of interesting people who were either quite outside the social grades or who did not seem to fit in, or choose to fit in, to any level. There was, for example, Big Alex McDonald, who had been the richest man in town and still bore the sobriquet "King of the Klondike". He had moved almost overnight right up through the social ranks. He had, in 1896–97, bought a claim on Eldorado Creek from a man named Russian John for a sack of flour, and had gone on taking millions from it. They still talked, in Dawson, of the days when his string of pack-mules would come into town, each animal laden with a hundred-pound sack of gold dust. He had endowed St. Mary's Catholic Hospital, toured Europe, been received by the Pope, eaten from gold plate, and was now back in Dawson, his fortune depleted, his claims worked out, but his name still magic. He was a ponderous man of great strength, whose mind and body moved slowly and methodically, and his whole effort was bent towards repeating his successes. He never did. Years later he died on his claim on Clear Creek, almost a pauper.

Another who didn't fit in was Joe Boyle, one of the most fantastic creatures the Yukon ever produced. Like Big Alec, he had moved at every social level. He had been a sailor before the mast and a pugilist, and had come into Dawson in '98 as a partner of Frank Slavin, the heavy-weight champion of Australia. The two put on boxing demonstrations in the Monte Carlo Theatre and Boyle later worked as a bouncer in the adjacent saloon, which was then being run by Swiftwater Bill Gates. But this was small potatoes for Boyle. Somehow he wangled from the government dredging rights to a huge seven-mile slab of the Klondike River, from the mouth to Hunker Creek. He had raised large sums of money, built the biggest dredges in the world (the first one had seventy buckets, each weighing more than two tons), and was now one of the biggest men in town, physically and financially. He was a huge Irishman with penetrating blue eyes, a round, red face, and a firm jaw. He ran the telephone company, coal company, laundry and saw-mill. Out on the Klondike you could hear his dredges whining away as they bit into the bedrock and churned up the river-bed seeking the gold the prospectors had left behind. Boyle seemed to have reached the climax of his life, but actually his adventures, which were to take him to the shadow of the Rumanian throne, had only begun.

Arthur Christian Newton Treadgold didn't fit the pattern either. He was an English public school master and Oxford graduate who had worked with a pick and shovel in '98 before going on to greater things. Now, he too was planning vast plans and dreaming heady dreams. He was part and parcel of the Yukon for all the time that I was there, and all of the time his name seemed to be on everybody's lips, and yet I never once laid eyes on him, though I often saw his photograph—a toothy little man, as small as Boyle was large, with a straggly, blond moustache. It was he who had persuaded the Guggenheim interests to invest in the Yukon, and for a time he was their general manager. But his great dream was to unite all the companies and all the individual miners into one huge corporation with himself at the head. In this he briefly succeeded, but in the end he, like Joe Boyle and Big Alex McDonald and so many others, was laid in a pauper's grave.

There were two women who also didn't quite fit any social category. One was Mrs. Robert McDonald, an Indian woman, and the other was Dolly Orchard, a former dance-hall girl. Both had achieved a vague status through marriage. Mrs. McDonald was the widow of one of the most respected missionaries in the North. Archdeacon McDonald had for forty years worked with the Indians in the Peel River country north of Dawson, and had translated the Bible, prayer book, and two hundred hymns into the native tongue. He had planned to marry an English girl, but when he went back to the old country to bring her to Canada she had refused to go. He had returned alone and married a native.

Dolly Orchard was now Mrs. Jimmy Turner. He was a gold assayist, and until his marriage had been a member of the social set, where he had been in great demand as a bridge player. They had tried to persuade him not to marry Dolly, but when he persisted he became an outcast. I do not think he had many regrets. She was one of the most ravishingly lovely women I have ever seen, with a full round figure that would have been a sculptor's dream, a peaches-and-cream complexion, expressive brown eyes and a halo of luxuriant titian hair. They made a contented couple and she achieved the miracle of stopping her husband's heavy drinking. But he soon left his job and they moved out on to the creeks to look for gold. They found very little and might have starved, but Dolly, I heard, made ends meet by taking in washing. I later knew many former dance-hall girls who buried their reputations upon marriage and made first-rate housewives. But very few invaded the sacred precincts of Dawson society.

Besides being a member of society, I also found myself a member of "the crowd who went out", as opposed, I suppose, to the "crowd who stayed in". This was also known as "the young crowd" and included anyone of any stature who wasn't married, no matter what age. There was indeed one Government man who was over sixty but who was still considered a member of the young crowd. The teachers, nurses, stenographers, unmarried daughters of established citizens, bank clerks, civil servants and "Guggies" all belonged to this set. The Guggies were those men who worked for the Yukon Gold Company, which was financed by the Guggenheim mining interests of New York, and who worked out of town in the Klondike valley colloquially known as Guggieville.

The crowd who went out went out every night. We went snowshoeing, ice-skating, sleigh-riding and bob-sledding. We went on elaborate sleighing parties. We sat on the side-lines in our best suits and huge hats at the skating rink, waiting for a young man to walk up and bow and ask, "May I have the pleasure of the next skate?" We went to fancy-dress winter carnivals, dressed as old-fashioned widows complete with weeds, or as French nursemaids in starched apron and cap,

49

complete with pram and dummy baby. We went on fast dog-sled rides with two to five dogs to a team, wearing long, heavy dresses and French-Canadian scarlet toques, and when the night was over we lay down in the moonlight and made angels in the deep snow. We were, needless to say, fully chaperoned.

There was always a smattering of the young crowd at the great formal dinner parties that continued to surprise me with their lavishness. We sat down at long, polished mahogany or oak tables, covered in net or fine Irish linen, and proceeded through eight-course meals served from Limoges china and accompanied by wines and liqueurs. We went from canapés to clear soup to fish to salad to wild duck to brandy pudding to fruit to nuts. There were always place cards, and specially made shades for the lamps, and the invariable artificial flowers, in great bouquets at the table, purchased from Turner Townsend (janitor and florist), who in turn bought them from the wholesale milliner-supply companies Outside and fashioned them into exquisite arrangements. After dinner we played auction bridge. There were elaborate prizes: sterling cigarette-cases, good pieces of china, sterling salts and peppers, teaspoons with nugget handles. In short, we lived to the hilt and nothing was too good for us.

Besides the bank clerks, and the civil servants, and the Guggies, we saw a good deal of a group of young Englishmen of the peculiar stamp one finds, or is supposed to find, in the far places of the earth. One of my most frequent escorts was an immaculate man named Howard Grestock, who, for reasons which now escape me, we always referred to as "The Bird". I have never known a man of such extraordinary tidiness. His moccasins were magnificent and he wore his yellow muffler with an air. His family were prosperous London jewellers and I suppose he was a remittance man. He never seemed to work at any regular employment. He lived alone in a log cabin, seldom rose until early afternoon, dressed leisurely and carefully, then strolled down to the Dawson Amateur Athletic Association, where he played poker until the small hours of the following morning. He enjoyed taking solitary walks through the hills and liked to squire various girls to various social functions.

A crony of The Bird's was Fred Chute, another Englishman of impeccable manner with a propensity for day-dreaming. He too played poker and occasionally did a little mining. He came into a title—a baronetcy I think—during this period but refused to use it. He tried to keep it a secret, but as usual the whole town knew the details almost as soon as he did.

Chute occasionally worked with E. H. Searle, another Englishman who was a member of the young crowd. Searle was the scion of a wealthy coal-owning family, a public school boy and a champion cricketer. He was now in his forties and his entire energy and fortunes were bound up in a mine on Victoria Gulch called the Lone Star. The hopes of Dawson were on this mine, for it represented a will-o'-the-wisp which all prospectors dreamed of: the mother lode. All the gold found on the creeks of the Klondike area was of the placer variety, fine gold washed and ground down by the glaciers, eons before. But somewhere, the old-timers believed, lay the source of it all, a vein of incredible richness. Searle felt he had it in the Lone Star and all of us put money into it. (I learned later that Chute had a great deal of money in it.) For all of my time in the Yukon Searle kept working away on his mine without success, his money slowly dwindling away, his hopes ebbing. His family in England kept writing to him, pleading with him to come home, but he refused to return a defeated man. His bones lie in a Yukon grave today.

I had good reason to remember Mrs. Ridley's advice in Toronto the previous summer about the need for a good evening dress, and to wish I had taken it, when the St. Andrew's Ball drew close in November. Miss Semple suggested that we both go down to Madame Aubert's on Second Avenue and try to get something, and we were soon fingering our way through the racks of low-cut gowns in her little store. I found a simple creation in the classic style which appealed to me and decided to take it if I could afford it.

"Very reasonable, Mamselle," said Mme. Aubert. "Only one hundred and fifty dollars."

The price staggered me. I was about to make a noncommittal reply when the door opened and two large, voluptuous women entered. They were elaborately but well dressed and their complexions were marvellous. I stared as Madame, with a bow and an excuse to us, fluttered over to them.

Miss Semple pinched my arm.

"Girls from Lousetown!" she hissed in my ear.

We beat a hasty retreat.

"I bet that brunette gets the dress you liked," Miss Semple said.

I could only murmur that the brunette could better afford it. I sent a hurry-up call to my artist sister in Paris to get me a gown and she responded later in the season with a suitable one of pink voile and lace.

The St. Andrew's Ball was a very formal and a very swish affair which followed the pattern of the other great balls in Dawson: the New Year's Ball, the Washington's Birthday Ball, the Easter Ball, the Discovery Day Ball and so on. Besides these, there were also ornate *bals poudrés*, when the entire town turned out in powdered wigs and eighteenth-century costumes to emulate the court of Versailles, so many leagues and so many years distant from the Arctic Brotherhood Hall in Dawson City.

The A.B. Hall was a big white frame structure in the centre of town, with a gallery of boxes, a large dance-floor and a stage at one end. All the main social events were held here. The St. Andrew's Ball began at nine o'clock with a grand opening march and did not end until five the following morning. I went, escorted by The Bird.

The grand opening march followed a punctilious routine. It was led, of course, by Commissioner Henderson and his wife, followed by the Church, represented by the Stringers, the law (the three head judges and police superintendent) and Mammon (the heads of companies). The rest of us followed along behind,

Everybody in town seemed to be at the ball, from Johnny McFarlane, the scavenger, to the commissioner himself. The butcher, the baker and every waitress in the city were there. The commissioner danced with one of his housemaids and I saw old Judge Craig holding forth with the scavenger's wife. For at these great functions all social ties seemed to vanish.

The men far outnumbered the women. They were lined up six or seven deep at the back end of the hall, most of them watching or waiting to claim the odd partner they had written down on their programme. Several wore simple black suits but most were in dinner-jackets or tails. We women sat on benches around the perimeter of the floor, our arms encased in long white gloves, our hands folded demurely across our laps with a fan between them.

We danced two-steps and schottisches for the most part, but there was also a Sir Roger de Coverley and a French minuet which was a great favourite with the Dawsonites. Almost everybody in the hall danced the minuet when it was played. At one end of the room was a huge, well-spiked punch-bowl which was kept constantly filled, and late in the evening the orchestra played the supper waltz, and we repaired to a separate room where an enormous meal was served. It was invariably referred to as "lunch", a name that used to infuriate the patriarchal and meticulous John Black. It was more like dinner, for there were great bowls of salad and giant pots of the ubiquitous baked beans and dozens of huge turkeys, which tasted rancid to me, for they had been kept on ice all winter.

Finally the ball was over. We walked out into the full light of the Aurora, whose blue and scarlet bars swept across the cold night sky. How strange we all must have looked—five hundred people in correctly formal clothes, trudging through the snows to our homes against a backdrop of shacks and log cabins and the dark bulk of the lonely hills.

Four

THE first wet fall of snow had come and gone under the late Indian summer sun, when The Bird invited me to go with him on a Saturday afternoon buggy ride to Bonanza Creek, a few miles up the Klondike valley. Here, eleven years before, George Carmack had found the nugget that touched off the Klondike gold rush. Thus, before freeze-up finally came, I had my first view of the goldfields.

The trees were already bare of leaf, but the yellow and crimson foliage of the undergrowth of aspen and birch and high-bush cranberry made a brilliant wayside fringe as we jogged along the gravel road that skirts the Klondike River. At the mouth of the Bonanza one of Boyle's huge new dredges was squatting in a pond of its own digging, noisily regurgitating the river bottom. Its high, unearthly whine echoed through the rolling Klondike hills.

Bonanza itself seemed to me to be a hotbed of industry. Log cabins, shacks, flumes, ditches, sluice boxes, surrounded by the paraphernalia and debris of placer mining—wheelbarrows, picks, shovels, and machinery of every shape—littered the banks and the beaches. There seemed to be men everywhere, all of them husky and in their prime, mucking with pail and shovel, tinkering with machinery, or more often just sawing up their winter wood supply. On the bare hills above us, as far as the eye could see, ran strange hesitant lines of yellow—thin horizontal scars cut into the mountainside for miles.

"Ditches and flumes," The Bird explained. "Miners built 'em in the early days to carry water to the sluices. Can't mine placer gold without water, y'know. They're a good six feet deep and some run for seventeen miles."

As we rounded each turn in the road, the scene was repeated again and again for us: the hodgepodge of cabins, facing every which way, strewn about the valley as if they had been flung casually there like chicken feed; the great piles of gravel tailings curving up the creek like huge tormented serpents; the bony fingers of the sluice boxes reaching down from the hills; the ant-like men swinging their picks or pushing their barrows or working their windlasses or hauling water or chopping wood. As we drove along we overtook brawny young men "necking" heavy sleigh-loads of provisions home from town (the traces passed round their necks). Others shouldered strings of ducks or rabbits they had shot, and we saw many old-timers lugging water from the creek in old petrol tins with wire handles. They all eyed us curiously as we passed.

The Bird, in his clipped way, explained exactly how the individual miners worked.

"First, you sink a shaft. Ground's all frozen, hard as a rock below surface, y'know, so you have to thaw it at night with wood fires. Haul out dirt with hand windlass during day. Pile of dirt—that's called a dump. That's all done in winter. When water starts running again, shovel dirt into sluice. Like a long trough, y'know. Crossbars all along the bottom—called 'riffles'. When sluice full of dirt you turn water on from ditch above. Water washes muck and gravel out of sluice but leaves gold caught in riffles. Gold's too heavy to wash away. Nuggets and dust. Now fun begins. Clean-up. Worth all that shovelling. Sometimes."

But already it was apparent that machines were replacing men. The Bird pointed out some larger outfits where steam shovels and self-dumpers were at work. The sluice boxes here were of tremendous length. In some places the four-inch nozzles of the giant hydraulic monitors were literally tearing the hills apart to get at the gold beneath. The once-peaceful valley was scarred with ditches, pocked with open cuts, choked with gravel piles, denuded of its greenery. Before they were through with it, Bonanza would be a grey, arid desert, ripped of its topsoil and its foliage and stripped of its mineral wealth, a great useless wound on the green Klondike landscape.

We were passing a roadside cabin and The Bird waved to two men who were working away outside. He stopped the buggy and helped me down. The two young men looked down at their feet, which were bare, and a flush of shame crossed their faces, for Victorian proprieties died hard. They put on slippers and invited us inside and thus I caught my first glimpse of a sourdough's log cabin. (In the years to come I was to see hundreds of these cabins and they were all of a package.)

The floor was of mud, brushed hard and clean, and the furniture was all hand-made. There were a rough table and two chairs under the single window, where the two men ate, and a home-made bunk covered with dark blankets, filling one end of the cabin. There was a shelf under the window on which reposed a row of old baking-powder tins. I thought this odd until I looked into them and found they were all filled with small nuggets or fine gold dust.

The walls were of log, of course, and without decoration except for a calendar and a bookshelf containing some treatises on mining, a set of Shakespeare, a volume of Leigh Hunt and some Kipling, for both these young men were products of English public schools. Over the immense cylindrical stove in the centre of the room hung a tinful of the inevitable sourdough. This was made from a thin batter of flour and water with a pinch of sugar and rice added. After it had been allowed to ferment, a little of it would raise a pan of biscuits or a loaf of bread as easily as yeast. It was from this concoction that the old-timers got their nickname of "sourdough" and no cabin was complete without it.

In the corner of the cabin reposed a row of petrol tins with wire handles which served as buckets, containers and general all-purpose utensils. I sometimes wonder how the Yukon could have been settled without them. Outside, nailed to a tree to keep it out of the reach of animals, was an old condensed-milk case full of food. On one corner of the table, as out of place there as a tin of *pâté de foie gras*, was a gold, engraved cigarette-case.

One of the men began to make tea while the other went to the back door and knelt down over a wash-tub.

"Ned's going to pan a bit," said the other. "He needs the price of an evening in town."

The man at the wash-tub took a large pan, rather like a frying-pan without a handle, scooped some dirt from a wheel-barrow, filled the pan full of water from the tub, and began to roll and tip it from side to side. Gradually, the sand and gravel slipped into the tub until it all washed away leaving three rather dirty little nuggets in the bottom of the pan.

We sat and drank tea and ate sourdough biscuits, and The Bird and his friends talked about some of the great strikes that had been made in the old days. I had heard some of these stories, though they were familiar enough then and are even more familiar now, for they have become as much a part of the Yukon as the "Shooting of Dan McGrew". There was the story of Charlie Anderson, called "The Lucky Swede" because he was lured into buying a supposedly worthless claim when he was drunk, for eight hundred dollars. The claim was up Eldorado Creek, not far from where we sat, and it produced more than a million dollars for the man who had to be tricked into buying it. There was the story of Nels Petersen, another lucky Swede. He was a cheechako (tenderfoot), and so green that he staked a claim on top of a hill when everybody knew all the gold lay on the creek beds. He confounded the country by taking gold from the hill-top by the bucketful. There was the story of Dick Lowe and his famous "fraction". A fraction is a sliver of land left over when two roughly staked claims are properly surveyed. Lowe was a chainman on a survey gang which mapped Bonanza and, after a good deal of persuading, he finally staked a tiny fraction just eighty-seven feet wide. He took more than six hundred thousand dollars from it, and The

Bird told me it was reckoned the richest piece of ground in the world. We could see Petersen's Gold Hill and Lowe's fraction from the window of the cabin.

"Now there's a funny business," said The Bird. "All those men—Lowe, Petersen and Anderson—they were all green tenderfeet. Never mined before. Yet they got the gold and the glory. The old-timers like Bob Henderson, who worked this country for years, they hardly got a penny. Ironic country, this, Miss T. You'll find that out before you leave it."

I asked our two hosts how they'd come to stake their claim. They explained that they hadn't staked it at all but had taken a "lay" on it from the original owner. This was a lease in which they agreed to work the ground and pay the owner a certain percentage of what they mined. Men would take lays on just about anything in the Yukon, I found. Once when the Bank of Commerce in Dawson was putting in a new floor, two men took a lay on the ground under the floor. In a period of hours they cleaned up thirty-five hundred dollars in fine gold dust that had filtered down through the floor-boards from miners' pokes. A friend of mine told me he was once watching a clean-up on Dominion Creek. He noticed that sand was dripping from a knot-hole in the sluice box and told the owner he was losing valuable pay-dirt. The owner simply shrugged, so my friend asked him for a lay on the dirt escaping from the knot-hole. This was granted and he got four hundred dollars in dust in two hours.

But the days of fabulous single fortunes won and lost in a season were gone. As we drove along Bonanza later that afternoon I saw on closer inspection that half the cabins were already deserted, their doors and windows gaping, their roofs crumpled in from the weight of unswept winter snows. As we descended the valley it came as a shock to realize that it was quite literally carpeted with the garbage of the gold rush. Here were rusty stoves, rockets, chamber pots, hand-basins, broken pieces of machinery, shovels, tables, boilers, gold-pans, bed-springs—everything imaginable left standing by the old cabins or flung along the wayside, so that the valley at a careful glance resembled nothing more than a monstrous dump. I never quite grew accustomed to this unnatural and somehow terrifying sight, though every creek valley for fifty miles between Dawson and Granville presented an identical appearance for all the years that I knew them. The spectacle haunted me all the way back to town, and then I realized that the town itself, with its second-hand stores and idle machinery, had some of the attributes of a refuse heap, except that I had become used to it.

By now, Bishop and Mrs. Stringer were well settled in their new home, a large, square, frame dwelling known as Bishop's House. I soon developed an immense respect and liking for Mrs. Stringer and began a friendship that has continued ever since.

"Mrs. Stringer," a friend once remarked, "is the sort of woman who immediately hands you a piece of pie as soon as you cross her threshold." It was a shrewd assessment. She seemed to be forever feeding people, especially Indians. They would come to see the bishop and sit for hours in her kitchen in their bright shawls, wordlessly accepting the unending stream of cups of tea and pieces of pie and plates of beans with which she plied them. When the bishop arrived, he would take them into his study, where they would, in their own language, explain their problems while the bishop listened gravely and respectfully. No matter how busy he was the bishop always made time for the Indians, and then, when they had taken his entire day, he would sit down at his desk and do his own work far into the night. There always seemed to be a line of Indian sleighs parked in front of Bishop's House whenever I passed. Mrs. Stringer called them "the roses around my door". The Indians in their turn had a word for the Stringers. Translated it meant "the two together", and it was fitting enough, for the bishop and his wife were seldom apart.

I soon discovered that Mrs. Stringer was a woman of great latent strength and considerable humanity. Nothing ruffled her.

Whether she was talking to the Indians, crossing the Rat River Divide, or shaking hands with the King and Queen (and she was presented on five different occasions), she never lost that inner serenity that marked her every action. She treated duchesses and savages with equal respect. I remember when she once quite unconsciously caused a tremendous flurry among the ladies of the Women's Auxiliary, because at one of the W.A. teas she sat Mrs. Julius Kendi, an Indian woman from Mayo, at her right. Mrs. Stringer, who never gave a thought to protocol, placed Mrs. Kendi there because she felt the native woman might be nervous unless she sat close to someone she knew. The other ladies were terribly upset, but if it had occurred to Mrs. Stringer that Mrs. Kendi was seated at the place of honour, I am certain she would have made no change.

A few days before Christmas a few of us accompanied the Stringers on what was to become an annual trip to the Indian village of Moosehide around the big bluff downriver from Dawson. The party numbered about fifteen and we drove down on the river ice in the great North-West Mounted Police sleigh, drawn by a spanking pair of handsome blacks. As we swept along the frozen river road, the bishop told stories about his life among the Eskimos.

"I'll never forget the time at Old Crow when old Joe Adam insisted I'd named his daughter 'Gasoline'," he said. "I had an awful time of it until I could get back to the Mission church and look up the record. It was 'Kathleen', I'm thankful to say, but I doubt if Joe ever changed it."

The sleigh drew up at the little Indian church in Moosehide. The Indians were gathered inside and here we put on an amateur concert, I singing something that I considered appropriate, the bishop making a short speech in dialect, and Mrs. Stringer, dressed in beaded and fringed buckskin, singing "Jesus Loves Me" and "The Church's One Foundation" in Eskimo. This latter was an instant hit with the Indians, who insisted on several encores. This done, a member of the tribe named Happy Jack entered dressed as Santa Claus, and distributed presents.

The missionary at Moosehide, who arranged these festivities, was an Englishman who had been in the country for years. The Bird used to say that every man in the Yukon had at least one good novel locked up inside him, and I dare say that this quiet, drab little man, who lived all his life among the Indians, was no exception. I heard just enough of his story to be intrigued. He had come to Moosehide five years before the gold rush—before Dawson City existed. They were lonely years. Finally, the previous prelate, Bishop Bompas, a man of fixed determinations, arranged a marriage between him and a half-breed girl of the village. She had been deeply in love with a miner from the creeks, but her father and the bishop were insistent that she marry the missionary. This feudal arrangement was carried out without a great deal of enthusiasm from either partner, but now, looking at them, I could not detect the marks either of tragedy or of bliss on their features. They looked, in short, like any other married couple after the tenth year.

A few days after the Moosehide trip, with a great jangling of sleigh bells and a great swirl of powdered snow, the fast dog-teams of the Peel River Indians whisked into town on their annual pilgrimage down the Arctic Circle to Dawson. They were a dramatic and colourful group of natives. Their dogs were decorated with great pompons of brightly coloured wool and their harnesses were alive with little bells. The men wore handsome caps bright with beads and the women wore intricate beaded shawls. They were magnificent-looking people, with long black hair of great sleekness, high foreheads, good noses, strong white teeth and a straight look in the eyes. They carried themselves with grace and dignity and did everything with a certain air. They wore jaunty buckskin jackets, heavy-beaded gauntlets and fur caps decorated with the tails of wild animals.

They were a clever, intelligent people, rather different from the Moosehide Indians. The women, I noticed, had an ingenious arrangement for carrying young children in beaded bags strapped to their backs. These bags were filled with fresh moss that served as a disposable diaper, and as they walked about town you could see the tiny faces with the black alert eyes peeping out from within their snug cradles.

But they were a child-like people, these Indians. They had come into town to trade, bearing flat bales of furs in their sleighs, which they sold to the Northern Commercial Company, whose store seemed like fairyland to them. Two things in particular intrigued them: electric-light bulbs and cameras. They bought dozens of globes to take back to their tents in the belief that they would replace candles. As for cameras, they went about snapping at everybody and everything for all of their time in town.

Their sleighs were parked for the most part in a long line outside Bishop's House, and later in the week, before they again turned their faces north, Mrs. Stringer asked me to help at a Christmas dinner she was organizing for them. It was held in a log building off an alleyway near the church. Here the Indians sat at long tables eating bacon and beans and stewed moose and not saying a word. Their table manners were beautiful and I remarked on this to Mrs. Stringer in some surprise.

"Archdeacon McDonald's training," she said. "Don't forget he lived forty years among them."

After the moosemeat they were given beef, which was a great treat for them, and fabulous quantities of pie. I played some hymns on the little organ, to which they responded lustily in their own language, for the hymn book had also been translated by the indefatigable Archdeacon McDonald.

Because of my musical training I was in regular demand in Dawson for concerts and at other events. During one period, I played the organ in the Christian Science Church, then hurried over to St. Paul's to sing in the Anglican choir. On Christmas Eve, along with the other choir members, I became a Roman Catholic. The R.C. choir was small and we always helped them out at their Midnight Mass, singing lustily in Latin as if we had been lifelong Papists. Usually the Presbyterian choir came along, too, but the practice finally ceased when somebody counted noses and discovered that the Protestants far outnumbered the Romans.

Early that season my music got me into trouble. A leading Liberal, T. D. MacFarlane (I suppose in a big city he might have been called a "ward heeler"), asked if I would sing at a forthcoming meeting at which the Liberal candidate for Yukon Council, F. T. Congdon, colloquially known as "The Silver-Tongued Orator", would speak. Another well-known Liberal, Billy O'Brien, would sing with me. I was delighted to comply, for at this point I had no realization of the two fierce political camps into which the town was split.

Dawson at this time was a predominantly Liberal town. The Liberals held all the Government jobs and as a result most of the prominent socialites were Liberals. So were many of the downtowners, as we called them. The Roman Catholics, of course, were all Liberal, for Sir Wilfrid Laurier, the great French-Canadian statesman, was Prime Minister. Although I did not realize I was working for the Federal Government until I got my first pay cheque, I was naturally suspected of having Liberal tendencies because I held a Government job and worked under Mr. Bragg, a strong Liberal. Actually, I suppose if I was anything, I was a socialist out of respect to my father. None of my Conservative friends minded this, for in those days to be a Socialist was to be merely eccentric, while to be a Liberal was to be damned for ever. Indeed, I once heard Mrs. George Black remark in all seriousness that she would like to see every Liberal boil in Hell.

Thus, when it became known that I was to attend, and indeed partake in, a Liberal meeting, consternation reigned among my Conservative friends. John Black was quite beside himself. He called on me at once, his voice shaking with emotion and fury.

"You do not know and you cannot understand the trickery,

the knavery, the crookedness and the venality that is behind the outward façade of this so-called 'entertainment' into which you, an innocent teacher of small children, have been so craftily inveigled," he said. "As your friend, as one who admires you, I advise—indeed I plead with you—to steer clear of the whole rotten bunch."

He kept on, punctuating his remarks with vicious movements of his silver-handled cane. He pointed out that in my capacity as a public servant it would be unwise for me to "appear to take sides by assisting publicly at what, call it what they like, is nothing more than a Liberal political meeting aimed at winning votes". He went on to add that, if I insisted on continuing with my "mad plan", the town's most respected citizens (meaning the Conservatives), who liked to think that teachers were above politics, would be rightly grieved.

I gave in. I sent my regrets and when the night of the big meeting came around I spent a dull evening at home.

And thus, with teapot tempests and minor alarums and excursions, the town settled into the long evening of winter. For all of November and December the temperature had remained comparatively moderate. Then, on the night of the New Year's Eve Ball, it suddenly dropped to thirty below. Everybody laughed when I referred to this as "the freeze". "Wait until it gets down around fifty or sixty," they told me. A few days later, the thermometer of our little house showed fifty-five below and when I put my nose outside that morning I felt as if I were pierced with hundreds of electric needles.

In such weather our excursions out of doors were short. The schools closed when the spirits hit fifty, and when I did venture out I piled on all the extra clothing I possessed, tying a heavy woollen scarf around the waist of my fur-lined Harris tweed coat, pulling long black woollen tights over my legs, and heavy worsted socks over my boots before pulling on my overshoes. My head was protected by a fur turban covered with a thick wool veil. Half my duties at school now seemed to consist of removing and then replacing the children's clothing. They all wore ground-length coon-skin and musk-rat coats which presented an incongruous appearance, for it turned them into tiny adults.

Strangely, I found that I rarely shivered in this cold as I had in the East, for there was little humidity. There was only one annoying manifestation. My eyelids were continually sticking together with frost, and my handkerchief, whether in my muff or pocket, usually came out frozen stiff.

It was not a severe winter that first year, but it was long and dark. The sun vanished entirely for almost two months, and when the temperature dropped lower than forty below a heavy fog enshrouded the town. It was a relief at the end of January to see the sun again, though the cold did not abate. By March, the temperature had risen to an average of ten below zero, and the nippy air, the bright sunshine and the dry, powdery snow made snowshoeing along the river trails or coasting down the hard-packed hills an exhilarating pastime.

In March, too, with the back of the long winter well bent, if not broken, the first passengers began to arrive on the Overland Stage from Whitehorse. The appearance in town of this vehicle, once a week, was an exciting event. In the winter it brought the fortnightly mail from the Outside. In the spring it brought returning townspeople home again. It was drawn by six horses and operated by the White Pass and Yukon Company, which also ran the steamboats and White Pass railway. It travelled the three hundred and sixty miles from Whitehorse by a forest and river trail that was dotted with roadhouses every twenty-two miles. Here the passengers, exposed on the route to the open air, could warm up again before plunging ahead on the next leg of the journey.

The publishing of the stage's passenger list in the Dawson Daily News the day before its arrival was the signal for speculation and gossip, and this March list was no exception. Every man, as I have said, had a story, and every name on the list meant something to the townspeople. This year, at the bottom of the list, we read the words "H. D. Stammers and wife". It was that last word, "wife", that caused the tongues to wag.

For nobody had ever thought of Stammers as having a wife. He was a civil servant who worked in the custom house, but he was excluded from society because he lived in a small cabin at the south end of town with a handsome and notorious woman of the dance-hall era named Montreal Marie. There were three Maries in Dawson that winter, if I remember rightly. There was Sweet Marie, who was very buxom and golden-haired and reminded me of a large pleasant cow. There was Black Marie, who was big and husky and heavy-featured. And there was Montreal Marie, who lived with Stammers and was pretty, dark-eyed and petite. She had borne him two dark-haired little girls and I used to see the whole family walking about the streets in a domestic group, during the September days before he had gone Outside. Before she became Stammers' common-law wife, Montreal Marie had lived, like the others of her profession, in a small log cabin in Lousetown, with her name plainly painted on the door.

It was she, so the report ran, who had raised the money for Stammers to go Outside the previous fall, as a treat for him. He was an Australian and it had been almost fifteen years since he had seen his family or his home. He wanted to go and she sent him. Now here he was returning with the fruits of that journey, and to one woman in Dawson that line in the paper, "H. D. Stammers and wife", must have come as a stunning blow.

He had not told his new bride about his Dawson family, but there were few secrets in the North, and she knew the whole story by the time she boarded the stage in Whitehorse. What she thought or felt or did about this news, nobody ever knew. With her arrival, Stammers moved back into the town's social graces. Everyone was very kind to Mrs. Stammers, and very curious. We teachers had her to tea one afternoon. She was a very young girl, of considerable charm, with large grey eyes, a pale, oval face and an expression of great sweetness and total innocence. She spoke in cultured accents and obviously came from an upper-class home. If there were complications with family number one, we never heard a whisper of them. At the end of that summer, a merciful government transferred Stammers to another field of activity. Shortly after this Mrs. Stammers died in childbirth, of blood poisoning. Stammers himself was shot to death by a hold-up man in Windsor, Ontario. As for Montreal Marie, she quietly went back to her little cabin in Lousetown and once again posted her name on the front door. Of the three lives that had become so tangled, I always thought that hers was by far the most tragic.

Five

THERE was another name on the passenger list of the Over-land Stage that spring that caused us excitement, and that was the name of Robert W. Service. He slid into town one day without any great fanfare and was soon to be seen weighing out gold dust in the teller's cage of the Canadian Bank of Commerce on Front Street. By this time his first and most famous book of poems, *Songs of a Sourdough*, was on every-body's lips and the whole camp was reciting "The Shooting of Dan McGrew", "The Cremation of Sam McGee" and "The Spell of the Yukon"—wild ballads with a Kiplingesque lilt written about totally imaginary events in the Klondike of '98 by a man who had never been there, and yet withal strangely authentic and true to the land.

Miss Hamtorf and I, having missed Service in Whitehorse, immediately made a hurried excuse to turn up at the bank for a glimpse of the man whose poems we had already committed to memory. We had thought of him as a rip-roaring roisterer, but instead we found a shy and nondescript man in his mid-thirties, with a fresh complexion, clear blue eyes and a boyish figure that made him look much younger. He had a soft, well-modulated voice and spoke with a slight drawl. "An English inflection, an American drawl and Scottish overtones," I told Miss Hamtorf. (I later discovered he had been born in Lancashire, raised in Scotland and had lived for a number of years in California.)

At that time most of Service's readers took it for granted that he had been a gold-rush pioneer, and in later years I was to meet many people who would insist that "Bob and I used to knock around the dance-halls a lot in the wild days." But this was actually the first time he had ever set eyes on the Klondike. He had been in California when the rush began and had no desire to go north. Later, when he joined a bank, he had been posted to Whitehorse in 1905. Now he was transferred to Dawson.

Service was never much of a talker, but he was a good listener and he got the inspiration for many of his poems listening to old-timers ramble on in Whitehorse. We now saw him strolling curiously about in the spring sunshine, peering at the boarded-up gaming-houses and the shuttered dance-halls, which had given place to schools, churches, fraternal houses and even a Carnegie library. He was a good mixer among men and spent a lot of time with sourdoughs, but we could never get him to any of our parties. "I'm not a party man," he used to say. "Ask me sometime when you're by yourselves." He seldom attended the various receptions or dinner-parties or Government House affairs which went on unceasingly, and soon people got out of the habit of inviting him. Sometimes, when distinguished visitors arrived in town, he would have to be hunted up at the last moment, for they always insisted on seeing him, and the poet, if pressed, dutifully put in an appearance. I remember how Earle Grey, the Governor-General of Canada, on a visit to Dawson, electrified the town by asking why Service hadn't been included among the guests at a reception. We had all forgotten how important the poet was.

There was one incident in Dawson, a few months after his arrival, that was typical of Service. There had been a murder in town and the hanging was scheduled for a certain dawn in late September. As usual, the scene was the yard of the Royal North-West Mounted Police barracks on the banks of the Yukon. Service somehow obtained permission to be one of a small knot of witnesses at the foot of the gibbet. He was a man who felt he had to undergo every type of experience, and it was this persistent search for local colour that gave his poems their authenticity and keeps them alive after almost half a century.

Service remained at the scene until the black flag fluttered up the mast, and then, pale and visibly unnerved, he moved with uncertain steps back to the bank mess-house, where he spoke not a word but poured himself a tumbler of straight Scotch and gulped it down. This was unusual, for all of the time he was in Dawson he neither smoked nor drank. He was a man who liked best of all to go for long, lonely walks in the hills or along the river bank, where, I think, he did most of his composing. We would see him occasionally on the A.C. Trail, swinging along athletically, looking a bit vacant-eyed. He was always cordial and pleasant, but he had no close friends, as far as I know, and nobody knew him well.

On one of his rare visits to our house, we discussed some of the new poems which he was preparing for publication as *Ballads of a Cheechako*. In his soft voice, well modulated but always strangely vibrant and emotional when he talked of the Yukon, he read me parts of "The Ballad of Blasphemous Bill". I cannot say I was greatly impressed, for it seemed to me a near duplicate of the Sam McGee story, and I said so.

"I mean it's the same style—one man's body stuffed in a fiery furnace—the other's a frozen corpse sewn up and jammed in a coffin," I told him.

"Exactly," said Service. "That's what I tried for. That's the stuff the public wants. That's what they pay for. And I mean to give it to them."

He was an absent-minded man, his thoughts always far away from the business of the moment. He danced with me once during one of his rare social appearances in the A.B. Hall. It was the custom at Dawson balls to divide the dance numbers by a long promenade around the hall. When the music stopped for this interlude, Service, deep in meditation, forgot to remove his arm from my waist. We meandered, thus entwined, around the entire floor, and in those days a man's arm around a lady's waist meant a great deal more than it does now. The whole assembly noticed it and grinned and whispered until Service came out of his brown study.

Service kept company with a pretty, young stenographer

who worked for the Government. I remember how he would watch the Government buildings from his vantage point on the hillside, and race down to meet her when she emerged. They did not marry. The report we had was that her family did not approve of Service. His wild verses upset them and, because of his themes, they were convinced that he drank.

By the time *Ballads of a Cheechako* came out, Service's royalties were paying him more than his salary—indeed more than the salary of the manager of the Bank of Commerce, where he worked. He quit the bank and took a small cabin on Eighth Avenue under the hill. This little cabin, surrounded by willows, with its long, overhanging roof and its pair of moose-horns over the door, has since become a shrine.

Here the poet plunged into his first novel, *The Trail of '98*. His habits became more erratic and he himself became more inaccessible. On summer nights I would often meet him rushing pell-mell down a hillside trail or see him starting out on an all-night excursion to the creeks. Then he would shut himself up for days while he wrote furiously.

He wrote most of his novel on huge rolls of wallpaper, and when he ran out of wallpaper he used building paper. Sometimes he used heavy brown wrapping paper. He was a voluminous writer and decent foolscap was not only expensive but sometimes, in the winter, unprocurable. Service simply took anything that was handy, and in that town there was plenty of wall covering. He used to write with a carpenter's pencil in a large hand, then pin the results up on the opposite wall and stare at his own work to see if it was right. The walls of his cabin were fairly covered with his own writings, long since famous. When the book was done, the poet vanished from Dawson. He made a brief return, two years later, coming in over the Mackenzie Divide by birch-bark canoe, then he left us for ever. He had written feelingly of the Spell of the Yukon, but he himself preferred the French Riviera, where for the most part he has remained ever since. And yet of the hundreds of writers who came through the North and produced whole libraries of books about it, many of them pioneers who watched history being made before their eyes, only this quiet, colourless bank clerk succeeded in capturing the strange mixture of magic and tragedy, hope and heartbreak, of which the gold camps of the Yukon are compounded. It is a tribute to him that his books sell nowhere as well as they do in Dawson itself.

By the time spring came, we four teachers, whose temperaments and personalities all differed so sharply, began to exhibit traces of a Yukon malady called "cabin fever", which had provided the plot for more than one of Service's poems. In its worst phases, cabin fever has caused trusted friends to fight each other to the death with knives, frying-pans or any handy weapon. We did not reach this point but we certainly did begin to understand some of the stories we had heard about what happens to people of the same sex cooped up for too long in a confined space during the imprisonment of a northern winter. Occasionally there would be a story in the *Dawson News* about a fight in the wilderness between two partners, or the police on patrol would bring in a prospector in a strait-jacket who had gone insane from living alone. The most famous story of all concerned a former Chicago saloon-keeper named Fred Fee, who fell out so violently with his partner in the early days that they decided to divide their possessions and go their separate ways. So determined were they to get their just portions that they meticulously divided everything into exact halves. They partitioned the cabin lengthwise, sawed their boat in half, cut the tent in half and even divided the furniture and the stove in half. Then they departed, carting away their divided possessions.

I often felt that it was only our three-hundred-and-fifty-dollar pile of cord-wood neatly stacked in the backyard and paid for in advance that kept us all living together as long as we did. There had been one nasty set-to the previous summer, when Mr. Bragg had let me have the school piano for the holidays. The others, I think, were put out by this favouritism and pretended that the piano was a great inconvenience. "Is she having that *machine* come in here?" I remember Miss Ruler crying.

By midwinter a real rift developed over the use of the sitting-room for entertaining our beaux. For in those filmless, cabaretless days the chief evening's entertainment for a gentleman and a lady consisted of a stilted conversation on a sofa. Unfortunately, when one of us entertained in the sitting-room we seriously inconvenienced the other three. For the parlour was also the sole passageway to the kitchen, which in turn was the sole source of water, hot and cold, and the passageway to a shed which led to the toilet. Thus, while one girl entertained her boy friend, the rest of us were imprisoned in our tiny rooms until morning.

Miss Semple won her nickname of The Belle with good reason, for it was she who most often commandeered the main room. But as The Bookworm cheerfully endured any discomfort for the sake of her idol, it remained for Miss Hamtorf and me to become the plaintiffs. We stood it as long as we could, then called a conference where with surface amiability we decided that each one of us should have the sole use of the sitting-room, if we so wished, for one evening a week. The remaining three nights would be open.

"Never mind, Blanche dear," said The Bookworm to The Belle. "You can have *my* night. That will give you two, dear."

The arrangement, of course, didn't work. Our friends got mixed up over the various nights, complications continually arose, and everybody laughed, and told again the story of Fred Fee. The Belle continued to monopolize the front room, sitting with her lawyer friend, Jack Carswell, on the sofa in complete silence for long hours on end. One night, Miss Hamtorf and I plotted a terrible plot against The Belle. At two o'clock in the morning I pretended to wake from a sound sleep and rushed into the sitting-room, where the couple was still sitting silently on the sofa. I shrieked that there was a burglar in the house. When the alarm was over I explained to The Belle that I felt it *must* be a burglar, for I hadn't believed that any man could be in the house at that late hour for any decent purpose. I am afraid the implications of all this sailed completely over her head, though poor Mr. Carswell looked flustered and dismayed.

At any rate, when spring came we decided to split up; and two by two, Miss Hamtorf and I in one direction, and The Belle and The Bookworm in another, we went house-hunting. (Miss Hamtorf and I were known in Dawson as "The Tall Ones" while the other two teachers were called "The Short Ones".) Relations were so strained by this time that neither faction confided to the other the results of their search. On moving day we went our separate ways with scarcely a word. Miss Hamtorf and I had rented a square frame house under the hill and had just deposited our goods and chattels on the porch when, to our astonishment, The Belle and The Bookworm drew up in front of the log cabin next door.

"What a box of monkeys we all are!" Miss Hamtorf said, and the four of us began to laugh uncontrollably. For the next year we lived side by side, the windows of the two houses not four feet apart. But at least we had two sitting-rooms.

The long Yukon summer was now upon us. Contrary to popular belief, however, it was not possible to see the midnight sun in Dawson. It was necessary to go two hundred miles farther north, to the Arctic Circle, to see the sun shine all night. At Dawson we watched it dip behind the tall hills in the north-west about ten or eleven o'clock and rise again about one-thirty in the morning in the north-east. During this evening interval, however, the country was bathed in broad daylight. We would go to a dance at nine or ten in brilliant sunlight and emerge next morning at three or four still in brilliant sunlight. We would play tennis at one o'clock in the morning or weed our gardens at midnight.

June twenty-first, the summer solstice, was a day of considerable celebration in Dawson. It was the habit of the entire town to climb the eighteen-hundred-foot Midnight Dome behind Dawson and celebrate this longest day of the year with an all-night picnic. We left town usually about ten, wearing the absurd clothes of the period, so unsuitable for mountain climbing. None of us wore skirts more than an inch from the ground, for the Bloomer Age had passed and slacks, of course, were unheard of. As it was warm we wore a simple white shirt-waist and carried a "shortie coat" in case it grew chilly. There were no roads up the Dome, but plenty of narrow, interesting trails built by those pioneers who preferred to live far from the madding crowd. Up we climbed, our skirts dragging in the mud left by the spring freshets, until we reached the top, where at midnight we amused ourselves by taking photographs and picnicking until three or four in the morning.

During my first summer in Dawson, the continual light disturbed me and I felt a certain kinship with the hens that had been shipped into the country one June and, refusing to roost until darkness fell, literally dropped in their tracks of fatigue. Because of this circumstance, Yukon hen owners were careful to put their birds into shuttered hen-houses at night and turn them out of doors again each morning. As a result, the price of fresh eggs dropped during the summer from three dollars to a dollar-fifty a dozen.

As a teacher I found the twenty-four-hour daylight seriously interfering with schoolwork in June. The children became restless and inattentive through lack of sleep, and it was a relief when closing exercises ended the term.

The social season ended, too, with the coming of continuous daylight, and Miss Hamtorf and I indulged our mutual enjoyment of long walks. These had become a daily fetish with us, for we considered them necessary to our health. One of our married friends met us labouring up the hill on one of these excursions and laughed out loud.

"You girls make me laugh," she said. "You tire yourselves out with your everlasting walking, thinking to improve your health or your complexions or something. And what good does it do you? Look at the women in Klondike City. They don't bother about exercise. They work hard all night, sleep all day, drink and eat all they can get and they're always the picture of health."

We had to agree with her. We often ran into these women as they strode in pairs along Fifth Avenue on shopping tours, and far from looking evil or jaded they were for the most part fine, healthy specimens invariably with a peaches-and-cream complexion. Their profession was tolerated by the police—as long as it was practised in Klondike City and not in Dawson—but they were not allowed to mingle at any of the community gatherings. I was at one concert in the A.B. Hall when three of these handsome and full-figured sirens, led by Sweet Marie, entered the place and "brazenly" (as all decent women agreed) seated themselves in an open box in the gallery. An undercurrent of excitement ran through the audience, but in a moment a Mountie appeared in the box, spoke a few words, and the women departed. Over these people—indeed over anybody who didn't behave—the Mounties held the threat of a "blue ticket": an order to get out of town on the next boat.

Klondike City, the restricted district where the painted ladies lived, and which was better known as Lousetown, was on the far side of the Klondike River and connected to Dawson by a splendid cantilever bridge. There was, of course, a good deal of gossip concerning those men who crossed the bridge and entered that forbidden but very sunny-looking land beyond the pale. During the bright summer nights, of course, it was impossible for any man bent on this errand to avoid scrutiny.

The little houses, as those virtuous ones who remained on the right side of the river could easily see, stood in neat rows and (as the wires showed us through field glasses) each was installed with electric light and telephone. The occupant's business name was plainly painted on the door.

Miss Hamtorf and I soon became consumed with curiosity to see at close range something of the set-up of the forbidden city, and so she and I, one summer's afternoon, set out on what was ostensibly a berry-picking expedition along the banks of the Klondike. But as soon as we were rid of the prying eyes of the town we faced about and, slinking along by devious paths and rocky hillsides, we reached the plateau directly above Lousetown.

Climbing stealthily, and a little shamefacedly, down the rough, bush-enshrouded bluff which backed the area, we soon found a secluded clump of shrubs from which we could observe unnoticed the goings-on below.

If we anticipated any shameful sights we were disappointed and confounded, for the scene below us was one of unparalleled gaiety. Indeed, it might have been lifted straight from a Brueghel's canvas. At the back doors of the tiny frame houses, the whores, laughing and singing, calling out to each other and chattering like bright birds, were making their toilets for the evening. Some were washing their long hair—invariably bright gold or jet black—drying it in the sun and leisurely brushing it out. Others were just reclining languorously and gossiping with their neighbours. Some were singing lyrically. All were in their chemises. Our eyes started from our heads as we gazed down on them, for these garments were quite short, scarcely down to the knees, and every woman's legs were quite bare. The chemises were also sleeveless, which seemed equally immodest, and cut with a low round neck. As they were made of coloured muslin—pink, blue and yellow—the effect was indescribably gay.

This cheerful picture was further enhanced by the comings and goings of waiters from the neighbouring hotel, carrying trays of bottles and glasses or platters of food covered with linen napkins. I must say that as the scene comes back to me now after forty years, and it is one that comes back continually —the bright colours, the cheerful sounds, the brilliant sunshine, the great river flowing majestically in the foreground and the encircling shoulder of the green hillside carpeted with wild flowers—it is more reminiscent of a gay Technicolor film than of the setting of the largest red-light district north of the fifty-four-forty line.

And so we left it, climbing quietly up through the bushes and out of sight, feeling unusually tired and dishevelled, our long skirts clinging to us like cumbersome shackles. We slunk home quietly and told not a soul of our escapade, nor did we mention it again to each other.

Six

MY FIRST trial year in the Yukon had come and gone, and I had long since committed myself to the North indefinitely. I was, in fact, enjoying life more thoroughly than I ever had before, and I had no desire to leave the shrinking town on the Klondike for the brighter lights of the restless cities of Eastern Canada.

I was now a sourdough, according to the accepted definition, for I had watched the river freeze up in the fall and break to pieces with a grinding roar in the spring. There was another definition which hardly applied to women, and certainly not to me, which held that no man could be a sourdough until he had shot a bear and slept with a squaw. The wags used to add, after he had achieved this he would wish he had shot the squaw and slept with the bear.

It was at my second St. Andrew's Ball that another of those small incidents occurred that was to have a considerable effect on my future. The orchestra was bringing the supper two-step, "Turkey in the Straw", to a triumphant finale and we were moving in to cope with the enormous "lunch", when Mrs. Henderson, the commissioner's wife, drew me aside and asked if I'd like to pay a visit to Granville the following weekend.

"Alex has to open the new curling-rink. Why don't you come along and give them a couple of songs? Charlie McPherson is going to sing, too, and you can play for him. With all this snow, the sleighing should be fine. We're leaving tomorrow and we'll be back Monday around noon. Alex will fix it with Mr. Bragg about your class."

I had never been to Granville, the mining centre of Dominion Creek, some sixty miles away, and I was delighted at the invitation. I accepted at once and thus was my life changed again.

Off we went the next day, a lively party in the police sleigh, with a constable as chauffeur, swathed in bear robes, sleigh bells jangling, and a fine spray of dry snow flying up from the runners. As we dashed along the frozen roads of the Boyle Concession on the lower Klondike valley I was reminded of a Russian scene in one of the old school readers: a pack of wolves yapping behind us would have been quite in order.

Granville lay on the other side of the mountain divide that separates the Indian River watershed from the Klondike watershed. These two rivers and their tributaries made up the area of the Klondike goldfields, and all the creeks radiated out from a massive mountain in the centre known as the King Solomon Dome. Bonanza, Eldorado and Hunker flow down the flanks of the Dome on the Dawson side, where they join the Klondike River. Sulphur, Dominion and Quartz flow down on the Granville side, where they join the Indian River. The old prospectors believed, and some still believe, that somewhere locked within the great ancient bulk of King Solomon's Dome lies the fabled mother lode, the source of all the fine gold washed down the mountainside by way of the creek beds. But if the lode is there it has never been found, though many men have broken their hearts and wasted their bodies in the search for it.

We slipped swiftly along the hard-packed road, past Bear Creek with its huge, snow-enshrouded dredge, past silent workshops and little white-blanketed cabins. Nothing seemed to be stirring in the Klondike valley. A mile farther on we turned up the busy valley of Hunker Creek, and here there was a good deal of activity, for the individual miners were hard at work hoisting pay dirt by means of hand windlasses from the bottoms of the shafts to the dumps, which would be panned and sluiced the following summer.

By four that afternoon it was pitch dark and we pulled up at the Gold Bottom road-house on Hunker Creek. This was storied ground. Here, in the summer of 1896, Robert Henderson, a tall, gaunt prospector who had been roaming the Yukon hills for years in a fruitless search for gold, had found a few colours in the bottom of his pan. He staked a claim, then headed out to the mouth of the Deer River, which the Indians called the Thron-Duick (meaning "full of fish"). Here he ran into George Carmack idly fishing for salmon with his Indian wife and her brothers. Henderson told them of his find and suggested they stake a claim, and let him know, in turn, if they found anything that looked better. Carmack found something that looked much better on Rabbit Creek, a tributary of the Deer, but he did not tell Henderson. Weeks later, when Rabbit Creek had become Bonanza and the Deer River was called the Klondike, Henderson was still working away here at Gold Bottom getting miserable pay. One day he looked up to find two men coming over the hills. They were the vanguard of the gold rush which he knew nothing about. By then it was too late for Bob Henderson. The Government recognized him as the discoverer of the Klondike and awarded him a belated pension —but that is all the gold he ever got from the goldfields. Now in the twelve years that had passed since he put up his cabin at Gold Bottom a lively community of several thousand people had sprung up and then died down again. Here we would spend the night.

At the door of the road-house the proprietress, Mrs. Endle, an American woman dressed in stiff white linen, greeted us. From her deportment and appearance we might have been entering a fashionable spa at an Outside resort. But the interior presented a somewhat different appearance. The road-house was an institution peculiar to the Yukon of the horse and buggy era. There was one every few miles, for the roads were heavy with travellers, all seeking warm quarters for the night. This one was fairly typical of them all. We entered a large room dominated by the ubiquitous sheet-iron stove glowing red hot. There was a bar on the right side, and around it, in circular wooden chairs, sat the usual collection of queer, unshaven hangers-on, who evaporated into the gloom at the rear as soon as the commissioner entered.

What rabbit warrens those Yukon road-houses were—and what firetraps! The Gold Bottom House, like most of them, was built of logs and had many old cabins stuck on indiscriminately as additions. Indeed, it gave the appearance of a giant mother cabin suckling a litter of offspring. On the other side of the main room, opposite the bar, a wide doorway curtained by heavy portières opened into the dining-room. A large oil lamp hung from the ceiling and its uncertain rays shone on a number of curtained doorways opening into tiny bedrooms, one of which I was to occupy that night. Other sets of curtains opened on to the steep, narrow stairs or into dim, alley-like passageways leading to mysterious premises beyond. As usual all the partitions in the building were made of cotton and paper stretched on wooden frames. A single spark would have turned that road-house into a flaming hell.

The following morning we climbed to the summit of the Dome. We stretched our legs on the top and looked out to the line of the Canadian Rockies marching along the horizon to the north. Were we standing on an untapped hoard of gold? I wondered idly, staring down the long flanks of the mountain to the creek below. There was no time to speculate, for we were soon sliding down the long, winding road along Dominion Creek. We arrived at Granville just in time for dinner.

Granville was a busy community, entirely of log construction, numbering about eight hundred people, most of them men and most of them French-Canadians. There were three hotels, two grocery stores, two jewellery stores and a novelty shop among the various places of business, and there were two or three churches, a dentist and doctor's office and a school. The town harboured among its residents the usual sprinkling of human curiosities whom one ran into everywhere in this country. There had been a stabbing shortly before we arrived in the cabin of a woman named Gypsy, a prostitute whose cabin along the road to Gold Run was one of the most notorious in the area. There was a strange creature named "Kentuck", so-called because he had been chased out of Kentucky by revenue agents for making illicit liquor. He lived alone and worked a claim on Dominion Creek entirely by himself. He had a great scar on his face that ran from his eyebrows down to the nape of his neck and he was notorious around Granville for provoking violent arguments about the shape of the world, which he insisted was flat. There was another curious man known as "Doc", who worked algebra problems for entertainment in his cabin at nights, read Shakespeare and the Greek classics to the schoolchildren in a quiet, cultured voice, and on rainy days carved swords out of boxwood and gave everybody fencing lessons.

A welcoming committee ushered us into another roadhouse identical with the one we had occupied at Gold Bottom, and after dinner we were conducted to the Bachelor's Hall on the hill, where the concert was to be given. Here about fifty men in their best black suits, and some half dozen women, sat and applauded dutifully as Charlie McPherson sang "The Road to Mandalay" and a man named Spieler Kelly recited, with great vigour, "Remember the Maine" and I, in turn, sang something called "The Goldfish" and then rendered Chopin's Second Nocturne in E-flat major on the ancient piano.

There was dancing after the concert, followed by a sit-down supper (or, as everyone called it, "lunch"), to which the Granville curling club turned out in force. As soon as the music began a man with a huge moustache curled at both ends and a blond Vandyke beard came over and asked me for a dance. He was wearing a rather ugly dark suit, a shiny stiff collar and a white piqué tie, which I later learned his mother had made by hand for him. It turned out that this was "Doc", the dentist-miner-schoolmaster.

"I'm not really a medical man," he said. "It's just something I picked up while I'm waiting around for something to turn up. I'm an engineer, really. I have a degree from the University of New Brunswick. I've tried mining, but without much luck, I'm afraid."

He then told me the story of his trip over the Chilkoot Pass and down the Yukon River on a raft in the early summer of 1898. Most of it consisted of a lengthy description of the wild flowers he had seen *en route*. It turned out that, in between working algebra problems, or carving out toy swords for his pupils, he collected and mounted botanical specimens. Again I reflected, as I had so often before and would so often again, on the strange collection of men who had been brought together by the call of the gold rush. Here was a man who should have been a university professor, mooning about the creek-beds of the North. Indeed, he told me that he had been offered a job at Queen's, but the message had not reached him until he was on his way down the Yukon River on a raft. I can still see him in my mind's eye, that winter's evening in Granville, coming across the little dance-floor rather hesitantly to ask me for a waltz. His name turned out to be Frank Berton, but I had no idea then that I would marry him.

We left the following day and were back in Dawson on Monday. The first news we heard on arriving back was that the Granville road-house in which we had passed the night had burned to the ground that morning. Remembering the kerosene lamps, the cheese-cloth partitions, and the red-hot stoves, I wasn't surprised.

Late the following fall I had a phone call from T. D. MacFarlane, whom I still kept thinking of as a "ward heeler", especially after the affair of the big Liberal meeting. He had been present at Granville when I played Chopin and he was speaking now, as he always did, with considerable flourish:

"Miss Thompson, one of the legion of admirers you left behind at Granville is now in our city and is most anxious to renew your acquaintance."

"The one they call 'the Doc'?" I asked, and was at once annoyed at myself for thus suggesting interest.

"The same. And the gentleman is even now standing beside me, impatient to know if you will condescend to permit us to call upon you this evening."

I did what many women do when they really want to see somebody. I said I was sorry but I was engaged.

But the following evening brought an equally insistent phone call. Would I please show mercy? MacFarlane asked, in his dramatic way. I really couldn't understand why the Doc himself didn't come to the phone, but he remained a shadowy figure in the background urging MacFarlane on. Miss Hamtorf and I held a whispered conversation and decided we might as well get it over with.

The two of them arrived, and during their call it transpired that the Doc, who turned out to be a French scholar along with his other accomplishments, had come to town with the idea of holding classes in classical French. Would I be interested in becoming a pupil? I decided that I would.

The Doc, or "Professor", as the townspeople now called him, had rented a little cabin almost directly opposite our own bungalow, and it was here that the classes were held. It was a strange idea, this starting to learn Parisian French in a northern mining town, and the make-up of the class, a fairly representative cross section of the town's upper class, was not without its humorous aspects. We had a judge who, although somewhat abashed at being found in school at his time of life, was very earnest about making a good showing. He was punctilious as to accent, which he achieved with much frowning and pouting of the lips. We had a doctor's wife who was equally dedicated. Not only did she regard the study as "improving" but she also hoped to use it as a lever to get her husband to take her abroad. We had a pasty-faced, stoutish American merchant who so seldom spoke in English that one wondered why he bothered to learn a second language. I think he wanted to be able to deciper the French catalogues he received.

The rest of the class included, besides myself, a very Scottish, very shy, miner from the creeks, who always sat in the background, his fierce black eyes gimleting each of us as we were called upon to answer the Professor, but who turned a vivid scarlet when his own turn came; and a civil servant who wanted to brush up his accent and who continually argued with the "Prof", as he called him, about pronunciation.

I noticed after a few lessons that the others carefully avoided the only easy chair in the Professor's cabin, for they seemed to feel they should sit in the hardest seats possible in order to study properly. "I don't feel I could *think* in that chair," the judge said, when it was offered to him, so it fell to me. Its comfort didn't worry me, though possibly my French didn't improve as rapidly as theirs. But there were other reasons for that. After the class, the Professor would see me home, as I was the only unattached woman. Soon I was calling him Frank, and when he asked me to go to the St. Andrew's Ball with him I gladly accepted. It was just one year since I had first seen him at Granville.

By now I was entirely woven into the elaborate social tapestry of the town and like everybody else was only dimly conscious that in the backgroud was a darker fabric imposed on us by the nature of the country. As we danced the French minuet in our Paris gowns, men were struggling and sometimes dying in the sombre hills and valleys just beyond. Word had filtered in vaguely about a terrible fight upriver between a man and a grizzly. And at the ball that week there was a gap in the Opening Grand March. The Church, as represented by Bishop Stringer, was missing. He had simply vanished into the snows on the trail that crosses the great divide between Fort McPherson in the Peel River country and the Yukon watershed. A wave of worry swept over the town, for he was long overdue and no word had crept out about him. Mrs. Stringer was Outside having her fourth baby.

And so we danced on, as the thick curtain of snow fell ceaselessly outside, filling the six-foot ditches and powdering the dark backdrop of spruce trees on the hills. We danced while the rising wind whipped the snow into great drifts and the husky dogs sent up a doleful howl that drifted through the snow across the little cabins from dog to dog, until it reached Moosehide, where the Indian dogs in turn took up the chorus and carried the melancholy message down the river to other dogs howling in front of solitary cabins thick with snow. We could not know it then, as we danced inside the hall, under the bright Japanese lanterns, but almost as the orchestra played, the bishop, lost in the mountain wilderness, was methodically eating his boots to save himself from death by starvation.

There was no word for almost two months—then a flurry of excitement as the bishop, looking gaunt and worn, came in by sleigh from Fort Yukon. He had a harrowing story to tell, and over the months that followed it came out bit by bit.

The route between Fort McPherson and Dawson City is a long and dangerous one, and those stampeders who had attempted to reach the Klondike by this passage had been as long as two years on the trail from Edmonton. It was said that for every hundred men who started on this route only fifty succeeded in achieving their goal. Certainly more men died on the Rat River Divide than on all the other trails of '98 combined. But the bishop was used to the journey and made it almost every year. His route led him up the Peel River to the Rat and up the Rat to the end of navigation. Then he would portage over the mountain divide to the West Rat and down that river to the Porcupine, which, in turn, led to Fort Yukon on the river.

On this trip the bishop's Indian guide fell ill and the bishop and his companion, C. J. Johnston, another Church of England missionary, had to turn back. Partly because of this delay the freeze-up caught them before they crossed the divide. A blizzard sprang up and the river began to run with blocks of ice, so they were forced to abandon their canoe and strike out on hand-made snow-shoes improvised from willow boughs and moccasin strips. Then with three days' provision—all they had with them—they started mushing in the general direction of the divide. Before long they realized they were completely lost in a maze of mountains, deep crevasses and frozen rivers. Soon the thick fog of forty below descended on them, obliterating familiar landscapes and seeping with chill fingers through their light clothing. To their horror, after each day of heavy mushing, the two men would arrive back at the spot where they had abandoned the canoe. Their provisions were exhausted and they were down to a single spoonful of Grape Nuts each and whatever berries they could find clinging to the leafless, snow-covered cranberry bushes.

It was at this juncture that Bishop Stringer hit on an idea for which he was to become famous, and which was later to inspire a scene for Charlie Chaplin's motion picture *The Gold Rush*. For years he had heard of and seen the Indians boiling beaver-skins with the hair off and drinking the soup that formed. The bishop and Johnston decided to accomplish the same feat with their boots, which had walrus soles and seal-skin tops. They scraped what hair they could from them and then, as the snow fell about them, built a fire and boiled the boots for seven hours, afterwards baking them on hot stones. They ate the result, which the bishop told me was tough and stringy, but palatable and fairly satisfying. Thus nourished, they again set out, but still got nowhere. Finally they decided to construct a platform and climb up on it to escape marauding wolves, who might have torn them to pieces as they waited for death. No sooner was this decision advanced than the bishop rejected it.

"I decided," he explained, "that if we were strong enough to build ourselves a platform to die on, then we might as well keep on living."

They trudged on through the snow until finally they reached a large river which neither recognized. The bishop broke the ice to see which way the current was flowing. It was going north, so he was sure he was on the Peel. This was heartening—and so was the marten trap they stumbled on under the snow, the first sign of humanity in more than a month. They ate the rest of their boots and stumbled on following the line of the river. Then in the distance they heard the sound of dogs and children and knew they were saved.

They were so exhausted it took them five hours to travel the final mile to the encampment. The bishop had lost fifty pounds and the Indians did not recognize him until he called one of them by name and muttered the single word *"iziquilsiz"*, meaning "hungry". Neither man could walk any farther, and the Indians who came out from the village to meet them had to carry them in on their backs.

The bishop told me that at first he found it very difficult to eat, and that even after he was able to take some meat, he found himself saving the bones and sneaking them into his pockets as a sort of reflex action acquired during those days when every morsel of seal-skin counted. When the two were strong enough to walk again they mushed back to Fort Mc-Pherson, where they regained their strength. This done, the bishop turned back again and walked the entire distance over the Rat River Divide in the dead of winter to Fort Yukon, where a sleigh brought him to Dawson. From this point on he was known as The Bishop Who Ate His Boots.

A month later, in January, there was a second flurry. We were playing bridge one evening, four of us, when Edmund Ironsides, the customs collector, called in. He had been up at St. Mary's Hospital visiting a friend when Jim Christie, who had fought a grizzly bear to a standstill the previous fall, had arrived, badly injured, but under his own power. He had been terribly mauled. I can still remember meeting Dr. Alfred Tompson later on that week, shaking his head and saying, "I really don't know how the man hangs on!"

Christie's story was as memorable as the bishop's, and it is still told in the Yukon as the greatest bear story known. The battle occurred on a cold, snowy day in late October as Christie, a wiry, grizzled man, was following the trail of a giant bear that had robbed his cache of moosemeat. He was climbing the river bank when he looked up and saw an enormous grizzly charging at him from a distance of thirty feet. Without turning a hair Christie unslung his Ross rifle and shot the bear full in the chest. The bear kept coming. At four feet Christie shot him point blank in the face. The bear still didn't stop. A moment later he had dashed the rifle from the trapper's hand, forced Christie's head into his mouth and commenced to crush it.

Christie continued to fight back. He pushed his right arm between the bear's jaws and dragged his head free. The bear sank his teeth through Christie's wrist, smashing the bones like egg-shells. The two of them began to roll over in the snow, the bear with his teeth now sunk in Christie's thigh, each hugging the other in a death grip, the blood of each pouring over the body of the other. Then the bear suddenly relaxed its grip and rolled over dead.

Christie was in terrible shape. His scalp was torn down over his eyes and his skull bones punctured. One eye was blinded. Both jawbones were broken and one dislocated. His lips and cheeks were gashed, his wrist broken, and his jaw hung down against his chest. He staggered to his feet, struggled out of his jacket, wrapped it around his torn skull, then twisted the sleeves to support his broken jaws. His cabin was six miles away but he was pretty sure that his partner, George Crisfield, would call in at a deserted cabin a mile distant. He headed there first, and using the bullet end of a cartridge wrote this blood-smeared note on a board of the table:

Dear George—I am all in, but will try to reach camp. Will keep to the river. You will find a dead grizzly near our cache. Good-bye! Jim.

Christie realized that the narrow valley of the newly frozen Rouge River, uncertain though it was, was still the best trail to his cabin. He struggled along for hours, tormented by pain and slightly delirious. During the final mile, almost blind, and staggering like a drunken man, he began to suffer terrible cramps in his legs and had to stop periodically to massage them. Half a mile from the camp he found himself caught in a canyon with open water, quite impassable, straight ahead. He now had to struggle up the rocky bluff, slipping and falling in his own blood and undergoing what he later described as "a struggle I would not endure again for nine lives". Finally he reached his destination, built a fire, and tried to force a cup of whisky through his broken jaws. The only way he could manage this was to mix the whisky with cold tea, pour it into a shallow basin and then place his face right into the basin and swallow. This done he rolled on to his bed of spruce boughs and lay there in agony waiting for his partner.

He waited five hours. When George Crisfield arrived, Christie found he could not speak properly because of his broken jaw, and in the gloom Crisfield took him for an Indian. Christie made him understand that before lighting the lamp and looking at him he was to take a stimulant. Crisfield, wondering, did so. Then he lit a lamp, pulled the robe from Christie's head, and staggered back crying, "Oh, my God, Jim!" over and over again.

Crisfield, shaken at first, recovered and began to search about for ways and means to move Christie to the nearest trading post, at Lansing on the Stewart River, fifty miles away. He and some Indians finally rigged a toboggan into a movable stretcher and set out with Christie strapped on to it. But the Indians were loath to move a dying man and had to be bribed heavily to go at all. The jerking of the dog-team over the mountain passes kept Christie in constant pain and his morale was not bolstered by the Indians, who had a habit of leaning over him and whispering, "Are you dead yet, Jim?" It was a four-day journey to Lansing and after the party arrived Christie's clothes had to be cut from him. For two months he hovered between life and death, unable to take any nourishment at all except soup, because his broken jaws had set in such a way that his teeth could not meet. Then with two other men he set out on New Year's Day with toboggans and snowshoes for Dawson. Despite his injuries, Christie spent as much time on snow-shoes, breaking trail, as he did on the toboggan. Seventeen days later he arrived in Dawson. The doctors looked at him and shook their heads. A week later he was sent Outside on the Overland Stage. (The man next to him on the stage was Bishop Stringer, who had himself just come through his own ordeal.) Christie underwent a series of operations over a six-month period which in the end mended his bones as well as his strength. Indeed, when the Great War came five years later, Christie was one of its heroes. He won a Distinguished Conduct Medal, a commission in the field, a Mentioned in Dispatches and a Military Cross. I visited him decades later when he was well on in life, a white, agile little man, living quietly with his wife on Salt Spring Island on the British Columbia coast, with only a slight scar visible on his scalp as evidence of that terrible winter when—while the rest of us were dancing in the A.B. Hall—he fought for his life after his famous battle with a grizzly.

Seven

By SPRING, Frank and I had what was then referred to as "an understanding", but I am afraid that it did nothing to narrow the rift that was slowly but inexorably growing between Miss Hamtorf and myself. Again, it was the Yukon cabin fever at work during the long winter months. In my years in the Yukon I watched many men, and women, too, share cabins together over a winter, and I must say that very few of them were able to continue the partnership for many years at a time. Frank's constant attendance on me began to irk my teaching companion, and I now began to appreciate, somewhat belatedly I am afraid, the unfortunate position that The Belle had found herself in two seasons before.

It was because of a secret fear of provoking Miss Hamtorf into an outburst that I refrained from serving poor Frank any refreshments when he came to visit me. For we were now acting very much like Fred Fee and his partner, dividing the food and the wood-pile and the living-room into meticulously measured halves. I really felt that an extra piece of cake or cup of tea or slice of bread flung to my beau would tip the delicate balance and provoke a scene with which I felt myself unable to cope.

But one night Frank ventured to ask, a little timidly I must say, for a glass of water, and I got it for him. It sounds silly to recount now how the two of us sat on the edge of the sofa and sipped this pristine beverage without so much as a dry cracker to go along with it, and it speaks well for Frank's persistence that this parsimony in no way damped his ardour.

But there was a terrible scene the following morning. As I

sat at breakfast, Miss Hamtorf entered holding the two glasses at arm's length. She placed them on the table with a bang and then turned to me and in a cold voice said, *"Well,* Miss Thompson, I think you might be a little more careful about appearances when you decide to feed your gentlemen friends some of our precious store of whisky."

At this outburst I became quite white with anger. I seized the glass and shoved it in her face.

"Smell it!" I screamed. "Smell it! It's water!"

Miss Hamtorf scarcely quivered.

"You've washed it," she said icily, and turned her back.

I really believe that only the merciful arrival of spring saved us from violence. How many other electric scenes must have been prevented by the coming of the equinox to that country of dark, depressing winter's night!

By this time I knew most of the background of the man I had decided to marry, and he seemed a good deal less eccentric, though no less intriguing, than the queer, bearded person called "Doc" whom I had first encountered in Granville.

Frank used to say that he didn't know who was the greater fool, I for marrying him, or he for daring to ask me on a hundred dollars and prospects. In those months before our marriage, when he often had neither the hundred dollars nor the prospects, I am sure the town was unanimous in thinking us both fools.

When he graduated from the University of New Brunswick in the early nineties, Frank had high hopes of achieving greatness and wealth as a civil engineer. Instead, the steamer *Portland* arrived in Seattle one day in 1897 with a ton of gold aboard and Frank, along with a hundred thousand others all over the world, pocketed his dreams, dropped what he was doing, and headed north. With the others he rushed up the Stikine River trail, had to turn back, tried again at the Chilkoot Pass, made it this time, built a raft on Lake Bennett and floated down the rushing Yukon to Dawson. But by this time the claims were all staked and the gold was spoken for. Frank finally staked some ground on Quigley Gulch, worked on it for an entire winter, but found hardly a colour in the sluice-box. Then he gave up the quest for easy riches and searched around for another means of livelihood.

By the time I met him he had done almost everything. He had washed dishes for a thousand men and cooked for a thousand more. He had been in the Mounted Police and had washed the skull of a corpse that had been recovered from the river in one of the Territory's most brutal murders. He had shovelled gravel into other men's sluice-boxes for twelve hours a day, seven days a week until every muscle cried out for mercy. He had been a school principal, a dentist's assistant, a stoker, a private tutor, a logger, a political scrutineer, a dredge-man, a watchman, a bill collector and a magazine agent.

"Frank is the cleverest man I know," a friend of mine once remarked. "He can do anything and he can make anything— except money." This was quite true. He could build a loom, design a pattern and weave the cloth for it; he could grind a mirror to the proper focal length, construct a reflecting tele-scope from it and gaze at the stars all night; he could build anything from a child's lamp to a twenty-six-foot power launch; he could identify three hundred species of Yukon wild flowers and reel off all their Latin names; he could read Beowulf in the original Anglo-Saxon, Homer in the original Greek and Tacitus in the original Latin; he could mush fifty miles in thirteen hours in fifty-below weather and he could cook any-thing from fluffy sourdough biscuits to marshmallows. But he literally never gave money a thought. When he had it he spent it at once on books or gadgets that intrigued him. When he didn't have it he got on perfectly cheerfully without it. The stars, moon, rocks, trees, flowers, animals, the splitting of the atom, the theory of relativity—for the study of any of these he would willingly stay awake all night, and often did so. But the mere making of money was something in which he could not get interested. Perhaps this was the thing about him that attracted me most.

All the same, with marriage in mind he did his best to come down to earth and try to accumulate enough funds to get by on. That summer he went to work as labourer for the Yukon Gold Company on Bonanza Creek, coming in to visit me each evening after a hard ten-hour day on the mud flats. When the season ended he got a job again at Granville as principal of the little log school there. But he was still broke and marriage seemed a long way away. In some climates, life in a rose-covered cottage, no matter how humble, may have been appealing; but the idea of life in a mud-roofed cabin at fifty below was only appalling.

It looked as if we might have to wait a long time for wedding bells, and it was while we were in this lovelorn state that an epidemic of whooping cough descended on the town. Dawson was almost entirely free of contagious diseases because of its isolation, but when one did arrive the school attendance dropped to a minimum. Mr. Bragg decided to close the kinder-garten for several months until the epidemic abated.

As it was more than three years since I had seen my family, I decided that with Frank away at Granville I would make a visit home. And so one day in early October, with the ground already deep in snow, I took the last boat out of town.

The last boat's departure was a considerable rite in Dawson City, for it effectively marked the beginning of winter. It was invariably a sad and sentimental occasion. The dock was jammed with people, for the entire town turned out for the ceremony of leave-taking. The last boat was always packed with the wealthy going out for the winter, the fortunate going out for ever, and the sick going out to die. The atmosphere was electric with brave untruths. Every last soul on the boat pretended to be returning the following spring, but in point of fact few ever did so. The last boat had a curious and depressing finality about it. For some reason those people who were quitting the country for good always waited for the last boat, and the last moment, before they did so. Thus it became more than just another boat leaving town; it became a symbol of the town's decay. There was always a forced joviality among those on the dock who called "see you next spring" to those on the deck, but when the final whistle sounded everybody on dock and deck began quite openly to weep. Then the boat pulled out into the river and turned its prow towards the south, leaving a little crowd of people standing on an empty wharf, looking cold and miserable and quite forlorn.

This season there were so many people leaving Dawson that there were two last boats to take them away. T. D. MacFarlane was going Outside—for a trip, he said. He never returned. Mrs. James McAndrew, colloquially known as "The Siren"—she had poured tea at the first reception I attended—was going out for a trip, too. She never returned. George Black and his wife were going out and nobody believed they would be back. So was my old friend John Black, who was on the other boat and contrived to send me a gallant message when we passed in midstream, "So near and yet so far!"

And thus we chugged slowly upriver, singing sentimental songs into the night, as the ice formed at the shore and the snow drifted down from the sky and the howls of Dawson's huskies echoed across the Yukon valley.

In Skagway I caught the Canadian Pacific Steamship Company's trim liner *Princess Sophia* and four days later was in Vancouver. I had left Dawson heavily clad in overshoes and fur coat and now I found dry pavements, green boulevards and sunny skies. I felt as awkward and as hot as I must have looked. Mrs. Stringer once told me how, under similar conditions, she caused a minor sensation in San Francisco on her first trip Outside from Herschel Island. When she went ashore she couldn't understand why everybody stared and grinned at her. Then she saw herself in a plate-glass window wearing her trousseau clothes of a decade before—large leg-o'-mutton sleeves and a trailing skirt, hopelessly out of fashion. Dawson, I fear, had some of the qualities of a desert island at times.

Many of my Dawson friends who said good-bye to me on the dock were quite sure I was leaving for ever, and I think that even Frank was a bit frightened about the symbolism of my taking the last boat. But I had every intention of returning, despite the protests of my family and the arguments of my Toronto acquaintances. By the time I received a telegram from Mr. Bragg announcing that kindergarten would reopen on the first of March, I was quite ready to pack my trunk and head again for the North.

Thus in the last week of February I found myself again in Whitehorse waiting impatiently for the Overland Stage to Dawson. It seemed like the middle of the night when the hotel clerk wakened me.

"Four o'clock, Miss Thompson. Stage leaves in an hour."

Four o'clock in Whitehorse . . . the mercury at forty below . . . a week-long trip in an open sleigh ahead of me . . . the little town dead and sleeping under its mantle of winter fog . . . a group of sleepy passengers huddled in furs at the White Pass station . . . the great sleigh with its four champing horses waiting.

Off we went into the silent night and into a silent world of white. For five days we would sit in this open sleigh, our noses icicled, our feet warmed by hot bricks and charcoal, while we crossed the Yukon Territory in a wavering diagonal line north. I have never embarked on a stranger journey.

Our luggage was limited, as it is on aircraft today, to seventy-five pounds, and my chief concern was how I could smuggle on some extras in the form of new clothes purchased Outside. (For my trunk would not arrive in Dawson until the first boat in June.) Fortunately I was slight, and I knew it would be cold, so I wore two suits and long coats, every pocket bulging with extras. These were topped by a man's coon-skin coat, which a friend in Whitehorse had insisted on lending me. The coon-skin coat was almost a uniform for stage travellers and every winter the walls of the stage office at Whitehorse were lined with tagged coon-skins waiting for the return of their owners from the south. In addition I carried, with as much nonchalance as I could summon up, an enormous black sateen bag which contained everything from a velvet Merry Widow hat to evening slippers. This the driver slung behind the sleigh.

It was not a comfortable trip. The seats had hardly any backs and we had not been out long before I became unpleasantly conscious of my neck. It just wouldn't hold up my wobbling head. With no support from the seat I tried tying a scarf over my turban, binding it tightly around my head. It was no use. I would just have to get used to the sensation.

There were fourteen of us travelling north. We sat in threes in two double rows of seats facing each other, the spare man up on the box beside the driver. I don't suppose if Dr. Gallup himself had been around to pick the passengers he could have obtained a more accurate sample of the Yukon's population from this sleigh-load of men and women.

First of all there were Grant Henderson and the new bride he was bringing north with him from Nova Scotia. Grant was the son of Robert Henderson, the man from Gold Bottom who had started George Carmack looking for gold and in this way started the gold rush. Grant was a huge man, following in his father's footsteps, still seeking gold in the creeks and valleys of the North. Later in life he was given an ironic job: the Yukon Consolidated Gold Company, which controlled the lion's share of the goldfields, employed him to carry its president on his back. The president was a diminutive, white-haired Englishman named G. Goldthorpe Hay, who came out from England periodically to inspect the company's holdings. He invariably wore morning clothes and a wing collar and it was Grant Henderson's job to keep him out of the mud. Fate was always wry in the Yukon but here it was at its most sardonic: the son of the original pioneer carrying on his huge shoulders the tiny creature who now profited by and controlled the destinies of the land which the pioneer had discovered. Grant had something of his father's stubbornness: he was one of those who believed in the tale of the mother lode locked inside King Solomon's Dome. All his life he sought this will-o'-the-wisp. All his life it eluded him.

Opposite the Hendersons on the stage sat a Mr. and Mrs. Ghat, who owned the hotel in Klondike City—the Rosalea I think it was—whose waiters we had watched carrying beer and sandwiches to the prostitutes in their chemises. She was a white, pasty-faced woman, he a jolly, fat little man. A couple from eastern Canada sat with them and the Hendersons. I did not hear their story until some months later. They had gone in during the early days, taken a cabin on the creeks and prospected vainly for gold. The land and the hardships had been too much for her and a few years previously she had without warning fled the country in the company of her husband's partner. Tongues wagged in Dawson but her husband acted exactly as if nothing had happened. Then word filtered back to him that she was destitute in Toronto, deserted by the man she had run off with. He made no comment but packed a bag and went out over the trail to bring her back again. Now here they were, for all the world like a honeymoon couple, returning to the land that he loved and she hated. Looking at them, I would never have guessed that a shadow had passed between them.

I sat in the rear seat, squeezed between a Swede on one side and a French-Canadian miner on the other. The Swede was a huge, gaunt wedge of a man with a great walrus moustache and a long nose and chin. The French-Canadian was round-faced, jolly and plump. At first I was only too glad of the fur-coated warmth of their proximity, for I was so cold I would cheerfully have cuddled a grizzly. But as the journey continued, I couldn't help realizing that the warm and persistent pressure coming simultaneously from both sides was not altogether the result of confined space. For five days I parried their advances, which followed much the same line.

"I mak' you present ermine skin, hey?" murmured the Quebecker, affectionately pressing my arm. "Two, t'ree, yes, enough for nice collar. How you like dat, hey?" Another squeeze.

Then from the other side—this time pressure against my

leg and the Swedish voice: "In Dawson you go mit me to show, yah? Ve haf a good time, yah?" To all of which I smiled demurely and maintained a discreet silence.

Across from me sat an English couple who knew Frank well and who were later to become our close friends—Mr. and Mrs. Arthur Coldrick. She was a plump, pleasant-faced woman who did not care too much for the Yukon and who quite often spent her winters Outside. He was the epitome of the transplanted Englishman. For all of his time in Dawson he wore clothes cut in the English style, a black bowler hat or cloth tweed cap, and carried a tightly rolled umbrella. He subscribed to *Punch*, *Sketch*, the *Tatler*, *The Times* and the *Illustrated London News* and remained, to the end, the complete Englishman. He had come out in the nineties and tried to do some farming in British Columbia, without much success, then had gone north during the rush. Although he left England before the age of the motor-car he insisted on calling gasoline "petrol", and elevators were always "lifts". On the winter stage, as everywhere, he managed to look as if he had just stepped off a Piccadilly street corner.

Next to the Coldricks sat a prospector—the typical, grizzled miner of fiction, unshaven, pale-faced, with long, untidy hair, a dirty white collar and a flask in his pocket. Up front beside the driver sat another mining man named Tom Kirkpatrick, who was very jovial and drunk for the entire journey. He had a bottle at all times and continually pulled on it. When we stopped at the various road-houses for meals and he could get no liquor he quite cheerfully drank horse medicine instead. Of all of us, he seemed to have the best time.

We sped across the white land, along a trail that had been carved out of the wilderness with axes and cross-cut saws and graded with ploughs and wheel-scrapers in the pre-bulldozer era. Our driver, an ex-Mountie named Webster, in his huge coon-skin coat and eight-foot red Habitant sash, held the reins in one buckskin-gloved hand and pounded the other against his shoulder to keep up circulation. The trail snaked from valley to valley, rose up over high mountain divides, took to the river, swept up the bank and through the birch woods, skirted giant bluffs, then dipped down again into the frost-silvered spruce forests. In all that five days on the road we saw nothing but snow and forest. I felt exactly as if we were flying on steel runners across the roof of the world.

We made four posts a day. The road-houses were spotted every twenty-two miles along the route and there was always a hot meal ready for us the moment we arrived, for the stage held to a split-second schedule. The horses were changed at each post and no matter how heavy the previous meal had been we were always ready for the next one. As a rule the driver didn't leave a post if the thermometer registered more than forty below. If there was no thermometer, a bottle of Perry Davis Painkiller, set outside the window and frozen to slush, carried the warning that the temperature was down below the danger point.

These road-houses were smaller than the ones around Dawson. In one general room stood the familiar giant heater around which was built an iron rack on which we hung our wet gauntlets, scarves and coats. Beside this was a long table absolutely jammed with hot food—roast moose, caribou, mountain sheep, native-blueberry pie and huge dishes of baked beans. As I was travelling alone I was allotted a tiny cubicle with a bed to myself. The single men slept in bunks, which in the smaller posts were all in the main room. I could never bring myself to undress fully in these premises, but always kept on my long woollen combinations and my heavy stockings. I feared fire, and if I were thrown from a blazing room into a snowbank in the dead of night, I wanted flannel next to my skin. Besides, the bedclothes were rarely changed and I had no way of knowing who had slept in them the night before.

The washing arrangements were primitive and the outdoor privies even more so. They were generous enough, to be sure, to accommodate a large number of people at the same time as well as a central stove, but the only division between the "Men's" and the "Ladies'" was a very short, very scant piece of canvas beneath which the men's nether limbs showed, unpleasantly reminiscent of the outdoor *cabinets* on the streets of Paris. Early in the trip I hoped that by being agile I would be the first comer to these houses, but I soon found that after a three- or four-hour sleigh ride most of the passengers were equally nimble. Then I tried lagging, only to find myself the sole female occupant while on the other side was a horde of noisy males, which seemed even less decent. At that it was better than the snowy trail. I didn't notice this alternative system until one afternoon, after the bottle had been passed frequently down, man after man dropped mysteriously off the sleigh, which slowed down for them. I became curious and was starting to turn about, when Mr. Coldrick stopped me.

"Don't look, Miss Thompson!" The command was urgent and self-explanatory and I closed my eyes on the instant.

By this time the male passengers could not by any stretch of the imagination be called attractive. Many slept in their clothes, few bothered to shave, and all wore, after the fashion of the day, long moustaches and in some cases beards, from which hung clusters of tiny icicles. When periodically one or another produced a flask and, after taking a healthy swig himself, passed it around, I feigned sleep.

We left Whitehorse on a Monday morning and pulled into Dawson the following Saturday. Our curiosity was aroused, the day before our arrival, when, driving into the small community of Wounded Moose, we saw a horse and cutter tethered in front of the road-house. The horse, covered by a blanket, had his nose in a feed-bag, but the cutter was empty. Then the door swung open and, to my surprise and delight, Frank bounded out. I had not realized that Granville, where he was teaching, was only fifteen miles away. To surprise me, he had given his pupils a holiday and driven over to meet me. After lunch he drove me on to the next stop, where the stage picked me up again. It was a happy interlude.

Mrs. Stringer and Miss Hamtorf met the stage. Miss Hamtorf

had given up our house and had been boarding all winter. Now we rented it back again and, all the vicissitudes of the previous season forgotten, moved our belongings in the same day. That evening I began to catch up on the gossip of the town. What an awful place Dawson was for gossip! The sudden departure of a single woman from the town was always enough to set tongues wagging and I am sure they must have said all sorts of things about me in my absence, though Miss Hamtorf, of course, did not tell me. A leading Dawsonite had been married and his wife, so it was reported, had cried all during their wedding morning and the following day the gimlet-eyed townspeople had watched while a pair of workmen trundled the double bed away and returned with twin beds. This was the main topic of conversation in the town, although a more sombre piece of intelligence ran it a close second: a party of mounted policemen led by Inspector F. J. Fitzgerald had gone missing between Fort McPherson and Dawson and search parties had found no sign of them.

As Miss Hamtorf and I sat and chatted a knock came at the door and there stood my Swedish admirer from the stage. Shaven and shorn, he was resplendent in a shiny suit, a high white collar and a green and red tie. I made an excuse about another engagement and he went on his way.

Two weeks later I was invited to Sunday-night supper at Government House. We were seated around the big table when the butler entered and touched Major Snyder, the superintendent of police, on the shoulder. The major rose, bowed to Mrs. Henderson, and went outside. A moment later he came in again, his face quite pale, whispered to his hostess and left hurriedly. She made an announcement that horrified us all and broke up the party. The bodies of the four policemen missing on patrol had been discovered by a search party. They had all died of starvation and exposure.

The party had left Fort McPherson the previous December for Dawson on the regular winter patrol between the two communities. They had expected to reach the town early in

February by way of the Wind River Divide. When they became overdue, Major Snyder sent out a search party led by Corporal Dempster of Forty-mile, and it was he who later described in his diary what he found.

On March 12, on the McPherson side of the divide, in the valley of the Big Wind River, Dempster found the first traces of the lost patrol in the form of an old camp-site, a couple of empty canned-beef tins and a piece of flour sack marked "R.N.W.M. Police, Fort McPherson". Dempster began to back-track on Fitzgerald's weeks-old trail, poking through the fresh snow with a stick until he located the hard snow underneath which indicated that snow-shoes had packed it down. Four days later he found an abandoned toboggan and seven sets of dog harness in a small shack on Mountain Creek. Inside the shack were the remains of a dog's paw and a shoulder-blade. This meant that the Fitzgerald party was out of food and reduced to eating its sled animals.

As Dempster and his men plodded on through the snow seeking the clues to Fitzgerald's fate, the story of the tragedy began to take shape. Here was a sack of mail, cached in the beams of a log cabin. Here was a toboggan wrapper and the remains of more dog-meat. Here, on the Peel River, was another abandoned toboggan from which all the rawhide had been cut. (Rawhide cooks into a jelly and has often been used to nourish a starving man.)

Then Dempster's eye caught the flutter of a piece of blue rag tied to a willow bush. Above the bush on the bank behind a screen of willows he came upon a grisly sight: two Mounted Police constables dead in their sleeping-robes. One had died of starvation; the second had shot himself. There were the remains of a fire, three sets of dog harness and a kettle full of half-boiled moose-hide. Obviously these two had been too ill to proceed and Fitzgerald had established them there and then pushed on with the other constable. All the dogs had been killed and eaten.

The following morning, ten miles farther on, Dempster,

feeling in the snow for old tracks, came upon a pair of abandoned snow-shoes. He climbed the river bank and followed the tracks into the bush. There, in a clearing, he found the other two policemen, dead beside their fire. Near them lay an axe so blunt it might have been a hammer, and not far away lay the remains of a six-inch tree chopped down for firewood with blows which must have been as agonizing as they were tedious.

Fitzgerald's companion, Constable Carter, had died first and the inspector had crossed his arms over his chest and covered his face with a handkerchief. Then he himself, his strength leaking from his body, had laid down in a hollow of warm earth beside the fire and died. When Dempster found him his body was frozen hard and he was lying in a position of curious alertness, his head raised and one eye still open as though he were scanning the trail for rescue that came too late. For McPherson and safety lay just twenty-five miles away.

Eight

WINTER gave way to spring, spring to summer, and summer to winter again. The first boat arrived and the last boat left. The river broke and the river froze and still Frank worked with pick and shovel and I waited in hope. Miss Hamtorf, with whom I had now lived for five years, left for a trip Outside. Her acid tongue had caused complaints among some of the parents and as soon as she was safely away Mr. Bragg dismissed her. I never saw her again. Miss Ruler, The Bookworm, was dismissed too. She had a sniffle which some of the more sensitive townspeople believed to be T.B. It was annoying, but I hardly think it was that critical. None the less she had to go. The Belle became engaged to be married, and soon she, too, left town.

Rather than seek new companions I moved in with two friends, Mr. and Mrs. A. E. Lee. He was a complete Englishman, whose sister kept a private ladies' academy in the old country. He had walked in over the terrible Edmonton trail in '98—the so-called "all-Canadian route" which many Canadians and Englishmen had taken for patriotic reasons. Mr. Lee told me that it had taken him two years to reach Dawson by this method, by which time all the gold was gone as well as a good deal of his patriotism.

Shortly after I moved in with the Lees, fate took a hand in our affairs. This intervention took an unexpected form: the general election of 1911. The background to this needs a certain amount of explanation.

I don't suppose the news of the Klondike gold strike was received anywhere with greater glee than in the federal capital at Ottawa. Rosy visions at once whirled in the minds of the politicians. Unlimited gold meant unlimited taxes, fees, licences, permits and jobs. A whole new territory was suddenly provided, ripe for patronage. A whole new district was waiting to be organized, officialized and administered. There would have to be customs departments, courts, telegraph offices, and postal areas, all calling for men to staff them. There were jobs by the score to be handed out, to Liberals naturally, for the Liberals were the party in power. Thus, during my early years in Dawson, every Government position, grand or humble, was held by a Loyal Grit, as the Liberals were then called.

Then, suddenly and unexpectedly, came the great Liberal débâcle of 1911. The Government at Ottawa was resoundingly defeated. What celebrating there was that night among the Dawson Conservatives! Within an hour of victory the Tories had every possible party worker (and some impossible ones) slated for the coveted jobs so long held by the enemy. These jobs included everything from commissioner to ditch-digger. The election results had hardly been posted before the Liberal job-holders were leaping aboard the winter stage and leaving the Territory for ever, many of them without even going through the formality of resigning. The next stage (or so it seemed to me) was jammed with Conservatives pouring back into the country. John Black, George Black and all the others who had left with me more than a year before on the last boat, ostensibly for ever, were now preparing to return in triumph. Not long afterwards John Black received a high Government post. George Black received the commissionership itself.

Frank had always been an ardent supporter of all things Conservative—clothes, manners, and politics—and he often told me of the hectic political life in early-day Dawson. Once he described how, during one heated election, he had, in the interests of Truth, Honour, Justice and the Party (the last word is mine), travelled on foot one hundred and fifty miles to act as Conservative scrutineer at the McQuesten River post. It turned out that here, during a previous election, more votes had been recorded for the Liberal party than there were voters. This suspiciously unmathematical result had caused the Conservatives to look quizzically at the Liberal-appointed poll-takers. Frank was charged with making sure that no further skulduggery occurred in future elections.

Now Frank was a prodigious pedestrian. When he was living at Granville and I was Outside, he wrote me that in order to get one of my letters he had hiked the fifty-odd miles to Dawson in fifty-below weather in thirteen hours flat. So I could easily believe that he had discharged his duties at the McQuesten River post with great energy, despite sleet, snow or blizzards. Surely now that the bells of victory were pealing he should be rewarded (or so I thought and said) with at least a minor plum. So, urged on and cajoled by me, Frank summoned up his nerve and, hating it, got on the band-wagon. He reminded the jubilantly cheering Powers of his own past efforts in the cause and was rewarded then and there with a promise.

A promise was enough for us. We decided to get married when the school closed.

We determined on a quiet ceremony. I felt that anything else might be considered ostentatious, for after all, Frank, despite promises, was only a labourer on Bonanza for the Yukon Gold Company. Besides, we both wanted to avoid the "shivaree", which was a noisy and often embarrassing complement to any Dawson wedding. After the ceremony every child in town would arrive with a petrol tin full of stones and set up a hideous noise outside the honeymoon cabin until the groom paid them off in dollar bills.

The only two friends who came to the ceremony were the Lewingtons. He was the mining engineer whose sobs I had heard through the telephone walls during my first night in Dawson. He was married again, to a young widow, and Frank and I had grown to know them well. We often baby-sat with their daughter Eunice, a clever and almost too-precocious child who sometimes used to startle the town by pretending her father was beating her. The North is uncommonly silent and sounds carry for miles, and Eunice's cries—"Please, *please*, Father, *don't* strike me again!"—could be heard quite clearly in every household. Most of the time poor Lewington wasn't even in the vicinity. Eunice also made a practice of crucifying her dolls. She was a dramatic child and I often thought she should go on the stage, and perhaps she did, but I have no way of knowing, because a year after our marriage the Lewingtons left Dawson for ever. We exchanged post cards once and then the ties that had bound us so closely together parted and we never heard from each other again. Dawson was like that. You could make friendships so warm and binding that it was impossible to believe that anything could dispel them. Then the last boat would leave and the alliances would end as suddenly as if the friend had died. Living in Dawson, I often thought, was like taking a cruise on an ocean liner. People would swirl into one's life, assume a tremendous importance, then swirl out again just as swiftly without leaving a trace.

Frank and I spent the first two days of our honeymoon in a small cabin on Eighth Avenue next to the cemetery of the Yukon Order of Pioneers. There was no romantic June moon, for the sun took its place in the evening and our only view from the window was that of the grey slabs, leaning at all angles, to mark the final resting-place of the old sourdoughs.

After two days Frank had to return to his job on Bonanza Creek. He had decided to take me with him, and we had discussed this before our marriage. There were some scattered cabins still remaining in the valley, most of them dishevelled wrecks waiting to be demolished by the approaching dredge, but as living-quarters they didn't appeal to either of us. After looking around, Frank decided the only alternative was a tent.

I was enthusiastic.

"A honeymoon in a tent. Perfect!"

And so Frank erected a fine new tent at the mouth of the

Sourdough Gulch at No. 67 Below Discovery on Bonanza Creek. With the help of some friends, he built a floor and a three-foot wall out of rough boards gathered among the tailing piles from old sluice-boxes. He named the result "Honeymoon Villa", and on a bright Monday morning, following our Saturday wedding, we hired a buggy and, almost swamped with boxes and bundles, drove out to our new home.

Bonanza had changed considerably in the five years since I had visited it with The Bird. The winding valley was now choked to the brim with long, undulating piles of gravel-dredge tailings. The pretty hills of Lovat Gulch lay naked and shapeless, torn to pieces by the great hydraulic nozzles. But many of the surrounding hills and gulches still remained unspoiled by men. There were wild flowers everywhere along the roadside— great masses of white bedstraw, blue spikes of wild delphiniums six feet high, masses of yellow arnica, and in the crevices of the older tailing piles, clumps of lupin and yarrow. Except for the clip-clop of the horses' hoofs on the gravel and the high-pitched whine of the dredge, the valley was silent. The day of the individual miner was past, and the horde of ant-like men, each working his own claim, was gone.

We crossed the little bridge that spanned all that was left of Bonanza Creek and turned into a narrow green valley.

"There's the gulch," said Frank. "And there's the tent."

And there it was, with a small Union Jack waving from the pole. It stood high and dry on a sandy knoll well within Sourdough Gulch and about half a mile from the road. On the lower side, half-hidden in bushes and mossy rocks, ran a gushing mountain stream. On the upper side, a steep wooded hill rose behind us. In the background the narrowing valley was lost in the higher hills.

But there was no time to sentimentalize over the view. The buggy must be unloaded, food must be cooked, a bed must be made up. Frank had to be at work by six the next morning. A busy week lay ahead.

The only furniture we boasted had been made on the spot by Frank in his free evenings before our marriage. The bedstead was made of sluice-box lumber. The spring had been found discarded on an old tailing pile. The mattress came from a deserted cabin. God knows who had slept on it before us. The creeks and valleys of the Klondike always seemed to me to be littered with rusting bedsprings and rotting mattresses.

The combination of the bed and a bed table made from an upturned box, we called the bedroom. The kitchen consisted of a number of crates and cases as closely and conveniently arranged as possible. The tiny camp stove we set up in the sand outside the back door. In what we called our living-room, at the front of the tent, were a deal table, a miner's chair and a home-made bookcase, all constructed without benefit of plane or paint.

With a foresight that now surprises me I had brought along a roll of green oatmeal wallpaper, a quart of green paint and a bundle of cretonne curtains. As soon as Frank left for work the next morning I began to paper the hideous board walls and the bookcase. The paint I used on table, chairs and bedstead, and in the so-called living-room I spread a fairly passable canvas ground-sheet as a carpet. When I had divided the rooms off with the curtain material, thrown a rug over a settee constructed of cases of canned goods, and installed a bunch of wild flowers in a painted coffee-can, the interior looked fairly homey. I still have a snapshot of myself sitting stiffly on a stool against a background of bookcases and flowers. I am holding an open book in the conventional pose of the time (though I can't recall I ever had a moment to indulge in the luxury of reading) and my seraphic expression is intended, no doubt, to represent romance and felicity.

It was in the construction of our bathroom that we contrived to triumph over our environs. Here Frank's engineering training was brought forward. One evening, tools in hand, he disappeared mysteriously into the dark gulch behind us. When he reappeared, pushing his way through the almost-tropical undergrowth above the stream, he was dragging a long length of canvas hose. Water gushed from its mouth.

"Where's that tub?" he shouted. "Here—I'll fill it up right now. And when it's full you simply turn the water off by letting it run back into the stream. Now, how's that?"

He had simply dipped one end of the hose into the creek farther up the gulch, thereby supplying us with an unending stream of running water, ice cold. I had all the water I wanted at my back door.

That gurgling stream proved a friend many times over, and occasionally an enemy. It was our refrigerator in the hot July days and we placed our perishables and meat in a box in midstream with the lid securely held down by a rock. Then one day a storm descended and washed refrigerator and contents away.

I did my cooking on a small sheet-iron stove set out in the open. Cooking in the open in the Yukon is fun, but only for the sand-flies, horse-flies and mosquitoes. I soon rebelled and had the stove moved back into the kitchen, where, behind a screen, I could continue my work in more comfort. Here I made bread, first trying the traditional sourdough, which wouldn't work for me, and then good live hop yeast, which worked only too well, completely filling the tiny eight-inch oven and turning my baking into a great charred mass.

I had one neighbour, Mrs. Dan Curry, a miner's wife who lived in a cabin down the road, and she lent me some proper yeast and showed me how to make bread, pies and cakes all in the tiny oven. She was a cheerful and helpful soul with no pretensions. She wore a ragged coat and when anybody remarked on it she always replied, "Well, I ain't lookin' for a husband, and I ain't lookin' for any political office and I ain't in society, so why should I get a new coat?"

The only other neighbour we spoke to at all was an old prospector named Smith Constance. We occasionally stopped by his cabin and passed the time of day with him. He seemed always to be in great poverty and the clothes he wore were invariably in rags and tatters. He was a former newspaperman with a good schooling who had come to the Yukon seeking gold, but so far had failed to find any.

Our groceries came out twice weekly on the local stage, from Jock Spence's store in Dawson, and I ordered them by mail, posting the letter in a rough box on the main road a few hundred yards down the gulch, where it was picked up by the stage driver. Frank was a prodigious eater, consuming great bowls of oatmeal porridge as well as bacon and eggs in the morning—and little wonder, for he worked a ten-hour day and a seven-day week of backbreaking toil. There were literally no holidays, and he had been hard put to get the week-end off to be married. For during the short summer season, when the water was running, men worked steadily day and night from spring until freeze-up.

Frank's job consisted of driving "points", a task which is unique in the Yukon and Alaska and requires some explanation. Almost all the placer gold found in the valleys of the Klondike region was in bed-rock or in gravel immediately above the bed-rock, usually twenty or thirty feet below the surface of the ground. As the ground was frozen perpetually as hard as granite to within two feet of the surface, the old prospectors had to thaw slowly down to bed-rock with wood fires. Later, the large companies used a device known as the "steam point", which was simply a length of pipe with a chisel bit on the end driven into the ground to bed-rock and hooked to a boiler that pumped steam into the earth and thawed it. Each boiler would be connected to five or six points and it was Frank's job to stand on a step-ladder with a sledge-hammer and drive each point to bed-rock. The points would pump steam into the frozen floor of the valley until it turned into a heavy mass of hot, jelly-like mud. It was not an attractive job, for besides requiring a great deal of physical endurance it was filthy and often dangerous labour. The boilers were always threatening to blow up.

Every lunch hour I would walk the mile or so to the thawing area to bring Frank a hot lunch and together we would sit on the grassy bank above the creek-bed and eat it. Below us we could see dozens of men working away on the shift, the steam rising from the boilers, the points protruding from the mud, the whole valley laced with a network of coiling hose, the bunk-houses and the big dredge in the distance. The dredge stood several storeys high and floated in a pond of its own making, squatting on a single leg—a thirty-ton anchor known as a "spud"—and swinging its bucket line slowly from side to side by a complicated assembly of cables that screamed continually, giving the dredge its peculiar whining sound. When the bucket line had reached bed-rock and dug its section, it would be hoisted up and then the entire structure would take a great, ungainly lurch forward on the spud—rather like a one-legged man hopping a puddle—after which the buckets would again commence to bite into the bed-rock. Actually, the dredge was nothing more than a huge mechanical floating sluice-box, designed to chew up the valley, wash away the dross gravel and leave the gold behind.

By midsummer, the crumbling little cabins had all been knocked to pieces as the dredge moved up the valley, and only one pretty little log house was left, marked by a lone tree like an oasis in the great heaving desert of gravel. This one was occupied by one of the dredge bosses, whose little girl I had once taught in kindergarten. Before the summer was over this house had gone, too.

When lunch was over and Frank back at work, I would walk leisurely back along the road-bed of the narrow-gauge Klondike Mines railway that served the creeks. The whole experience should have been an idyllic one, I suppose, but to tell the truth I was terrified almost every moment of my stay in Sourdough Gulch. More than once, then and later, I had cause to reflect on the truth of the adage that the Klondike was a man's country. There seemed to me to be one recurring theme in the tragic little domestic dramas that were woven into the fabric of the land, and that was the theme of woman against nature. I thought again of the couple on the stage whose marriage had been broken up by the country; and of John Black living alone in Dawson because his wife could not stand the land, and of Archdeacon MacDonald and the fiancée who refused to go back with him to the Peel River. The men all loved the country, but I do not think many of the women really did. The utter silence of the creek valley, the brooding, unknown woods behind our tent, the strange, furry animals that rustled underfoot and the strange, bearded men who occasionally shuffled by, all these things were part of Frank's life, but I must say they unnerved me. I had been brought up by parents steeped in the Victorian Tradition and early in life they had perhaps unconsciously inculcated in me the deadly fear of two bogies: first, a strange Man who might do dreadful things to me, and, second, The Woods, where dreadful things might happen. Now here I was, surrounded on all sides by vast quantities of both.

Not far from the gulch were several queer old men who had lived too long alone in their cabins to be entirely balanced. I am sure that most of them were as harmless as kittens but the sight of them sent chills of apprehension down my spine. One went past my door every morning with a gun in his hand and what I judged to be an Evil Eye which pierced me as I worked outside scrubbing out Frank's long, grimy underwear. His name was "Old McGillivray" but he was better known as Peeping Tom. Years later he was caught staring into a woman's bedroom as she was undressing, and the police gave him a blue ticket to leave town.

Another passer-by was really strange—a small, stooped creature with long hair and tattered clothes who walked by, never looking to right or to left, but muttering wildly to himself, swinging an axe as he went. He fancied himself an astronomer and he had surrounded his neat little cabin with long poles so arranged as to point heavenward at various stars and planets at different angles, each held in place by many ropes and guy wires. His face was pale and his eyes bulged, and the memory of him still makes me shiver a little.

Behind the cabin lay the dark hollow of Sourdough Gulch, into whose mysterious labyrinth of vines and matted shrubs I never ventured. Somewhere up there, the men on the points said, was a bear. One or two had seen it in the distance through field-glasses. I never investigated the matter and the bear, thank God, never investigated me.

One day I climbed a rock hill farther up the valley on a search for low-bush cranberries, of which Frank was fond. I realized at once that my cotton house-dress would be useless for this kind of excursion so I donned a pair of Frank's khaki overalls, a daring licence for a woman in those pre-war days. I followed a faint trail up the hill and my feet soon sank into a thick carpet of bright bear berries and kinnikinnik, a green, red-berried creeper sometimes called Yukon holly. I was soon filling my pail with cranberries, and was about to venture down again when a shot rang out, as they say, and a bullet whizzed across my head. I sank to the ground, every nerve taut, convinced that one of the crazy men had come for me at last. But there was no further sound and after an hour of quivering among the berry bushes I made my way home as swiftly and stealthily as possible.

A short time later Frank arrived back, obviously excited, and made straight for his gun hanging on the tent pole. "No time to eat now," he said, loading it hurriedly. "One of the boys spotted a caribou over on the hill this afternoon. Took a shot at it but missed. Couldn't follow it up—had to go on shift—so I'm going to have a look around. Maybe a young one; the noise from the dredge usually keeps them away." Off he went, and I let him go, but I never again ventured on the hill in a pair of khaki overalls.

And so the short Yukon summer merged into fall. By September the trees were yellow again and Frank had to break ice on the water in the basin to wash in the morning. The valley was full of fog and there was white frost on the foliage.

We shivered in our tent and wondered whether the promise made that spring would be fulfilled. The long Yukon winter would soon be upon us and the dredge forced to shut down. What then?

Our worries were groundless. In late September, when the flocks of wild geese were honking overhead and the ice growing thicker on the edges of our reservoir and the tent leaking more profusely at every rainfall, the word came. Frank had been appointed mining recorder at the Dawson City office. Our strenuous honeymoon was over. We pulled up stakes, sent to town for a buggy, gave a last, long look at Sourdough Gulch and drove back to civilization.

Nine

DAWSON was still shrinking, its population trickling from it like water from a leaky barrel. There were now not more than two thousand people left in town, and fewer than that in the winter. As the last boats fled upriver before the freeze-up, sudden decisions were made to quit everything and escape before winter sealed the town off from the world. It was as if people were escaping from a foundering ocean vessel. They left everything behind except for bare necessities. In point of fact, freight rates were too high to transport many worldly goods away.

On returning to town we were able to buy from a departing teamster's wife a fully furnished home for just seven hundred dollars. The price was a pretty good indication of the fall of a city where business property had once sold for as high as five thousand dollars a front foot. The furnishings included everything, right down to the pots and pans and two freshly cooked hams in the kitchen. There was a bin full of flour and half a cake in the pantry and every article of staple food needed to set up housekeeping. There were cupboards jammed with kitchen utensils, a new Brussels carpet on the sitting-room floor, an Ostermoor mattress and good linen sheets on the bed and a real eiderdown. There was a bathroom crammed with every imaginable variety of patent medicine, perfume, soap and toilet article. (The name was misleading, however, for this room contained neither bath nor toilet. The kitchen and shed served for these conveniences.) There were stacks of furniture in every room and more piled up in the shed. There was a wonderful armchair, the most comfortable I have ever known. After forty years I still possess it. It has been dragged from city to city and house to house and it is as comfortable as ever. The woman we bought the house from had simply left with the clothes on her back as if she were haunted by the plague. She had not even bothered to take her letters and photographs. Such was the Dawson of 1912, an expiring town on the banks of the Klondike.

Yet in the twenty-five years I lived there, I never thought of Dawson as a ghost town, and I would have been annoyed and flabbergasted if anyone had called it that. It had been built for thirty thousand people and now it held one-fifteenth that number. Its sidewalks were rickety, its ditches clogged with weeds, its cabins decrepit, its buildings leaning at all angles, its stores and shops boarded up or torn down, its grave-yard full and its houses empty. But after a season on Sourdough Gulch it seemed the very core of civilization. From our verandah we could see the whole town spread out checkerboard fashion, with the river beyond, and it looked to me like a big city.

I now donned my white kid gloves and began again the restless cycle of receptions around which the town's social life revolved. Before the month of October I had given one myself and the result was mathematically a social success. On these occasions we did indeed seem to be living a metropolitan life, until we opened the *Dawson News* to read that a wild-cat had floated down the river on a log, climbed ashore in front of the Green Tree Hotel, entered room Number 12 and viciously attacked the slumbering occupant. Then we were forcibly reminded that the wild stretched out in all directions for hundreds of unbroken miles.

Emboldened by the success of my reception, I determined to hold a dinner-party in the best Dawson style. The cateress I had hired couldn't come at the last moment and I was referred to a cook downtown, who sent along a voluptuous but sullen-looking young Negro woman who answered only to the name of Sally. She had not been in the kitchen five minutes before I

It was an unwritten rule that the teachers would live together, for no woman could live by herself in Dawson City and maintain her self-respect. (l to r: Donna Goodhand as Miss Ruler; Leueen Willoughby as Laura; Angela Fusco as Miss Hamtorf; Lenore Zann as Miss Semple. Photo: CBC)

I Married the Klondike

A CBC television drama

Top: Frank worked a ten-hour day and a seven-day week from spring until freeze-up. (Photo: Peter Kelly)

Bottom: It didn't pay to bring in anything but t[h]e best, and the stores were stocked with top-gr[ade] caviar, lobster and shrimp. (Photo: Peter Kelly[)]

I donned a pair of Frank's overalls, a daring licence for a woman in those pre-war days, to go on a search for low-bush cranberries. (Leueen Willoughby as Laura. Photo: Peter Kelly)

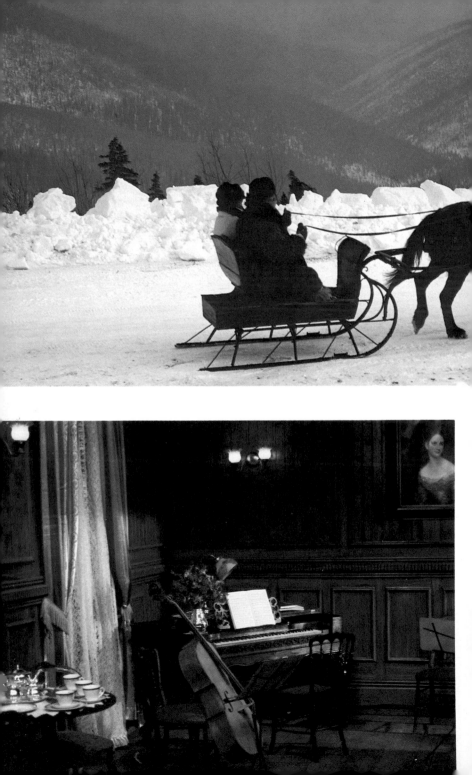

Bottom Left: Within this motley collection of log cabins and rickety frame dwellings, the most elaborate events proceeded in the grandest Edwardian style..(Photo: Peter Kelly)

Bottom Right: The sluice boxes were of tremendous length. The giant hydraulic monitors were tearing the hills apart to get at the gold beneath. (Photo: Peter Kelly)

Overleaf: The scene at Lousetown was one of unparalleled gaiety. Indeed it might have been lifted straight from a Breughel canvas. (Photo: Peter Kelly)

Frank used to say that he didn't know who was the greater fool, I for marrying him, or he for daring to ask me on a hundred dollars and prospects. The town was unanimous in thinking us both fools.

Leueen Willoughby as Laura and R.H. Thomson as Frank Berton (Photo: CBC)

realized with sinking spirits that she knew little about cooking and even less about serving.

I was miserable. Our guests included the cream of Dawson society: the new commissioner and his wife, Mr. and Mrs. George Black, the new superintendent of the police, Major Moodie and his wife, and the presiding judge, my old friend John Black. When Sally first entered the room I thought I saw a look of dismay cross J. B.'s face, and from then on the acting judge's features assumed a quizzical expression whenever he saw her.

It was a wretched party. The food was ruined, the little room stifling hot, the conversation forced. Sally was impossible. I almost groaned when she brought in the potatoes, which I had hoped would be light and fluffy and served in a silver casserole. Instead they were flattened out into a cold soup plate and sprinkled with heavily grated cheese. But it was the ice cream that finished me. In place of the pretty etched glasses I had laid out, it was served in tea cups. After the ordeal was over, I learned the reason for John Black's curious expression. Sally had been brought before him in court the previous day as a particularly undesirable prostitute and he had given her a blue ticket to get out of town.

The George Blacks were now the town's first citizens. Mrs. Black had become, by virtue of her husband's position, the arbiter of our social life. She was, by all odds, the smartest-looking woman in Dawson. I never once saw her dishevelled. She once told me that she had walked in over the trail dressed in top fashion, in Russian-leather boots with elk-hide soles, an ankle-length skirt of brown corduroy velvet, a Norfolk jacket and a natty straw sailor hat. In the mornings in Dawson she wore the crispest of ginghams and in the evenings the most expensive of gowns, purchased from Madame Aubert's at five hundred dollars apiece. On the hills out hunting with her husband, she was always dressed in the correct khaki outfit and she was never seen without a hat. She wore these hats at a rakish angle, pulled down low over one eye, her hair tightly close to her head. I once remarked on a particularly vivid scarlet toque she was wearing. "I've got *two* of them!" she said, in her emphatic manner. "I love hats. I only wish I could wear a hat in my coffin."

It was a bizarre remark, but Mrs. Black liked to create an effect. She peppered her speech with hells and damns and always seemed to be in the middle of some controversy. She once made a point of holding a tea at which she had the daughter of her washerwoman "pass", an honour usually reserved for the socially elite. There were cries of outrage over this. "Well, why not?" Mrs. Black retorted when she heard about the fuss. "My father was a washer*man*!" This was technically true, I suppose, for he had owned several scores of laundries in the United States.

Impasses of this nature delighted her. The only time I ever met Diamond Tooth Gertie, one of the most famous of the dance-hall girls, was at an evening party at Mrs. Black's. Gertie had married one of the town's leading lawyers, a prominent Conservative and an old friend of George Black, from the Maritimes. The Blacks were always loyal to their friends and I am sure that Mrs. Black got added enjoyment by breaking the accepted social code that former dance-hall girls were beyond the pale. Gertie was a demure little woman, quite pretty and very self-effacing. She had little to say, but when she did speak, the famous diamond could be seen glittering between her two front teeth. Tongues wagged furiously the next day. "The idea—bringing *that* woman to Government House!" a Liberal friend remarked. But Mrs. Black never retreated an inch. Once, at an election meeting for the Yukon Council in the A.B. Hall, George Black rose to speak. "They'll never let that man speak," cried a woman in the audience. Up stood Mrs. Black. "That man will speak if he has to stand there until Hell freezes over," she said. And he did. Decades later, when George took ill, she campaigned and went to Parliament in his stead.

Shortly after they were settled in Government House, the Blacks held an enormous reception to which the entire town seemed to have been invited. After the select gatherings of the previous regime, this was democracy in its broadest sense. The affair began at eight o'clock and went on until five the following morning. The building was literally jammed from cellar to attic. The place was full of miners, all friends of George Black. There were miners in evening dress, miners in morning dress, miners in overalls and even miners in gum-boots. One friend of mine, seeing a man she didn't recognize, asked a police captain if he knew him. "Certainly, Madame," came the answer. "That's Spot Cash Smith. He's just out after serving a three-month sentence in the Dawson jail."

The new Government House, rebuilt after its fire, was a handsome three-storey colonial edifice, with wide verandahs and wide staircases down which guests used to toboggan on tea-trays in the Edwardian fashion. It had a dazzling interior of white pillars and gold wallpaper and rich mahogany and walnut panelling and was easily the most luxurious building in town.

Mrs. Black engineered the reception herself, ordering a thousand sandwiches, forty cakes, twenty gallons of sherbet and an equal amount of salad and home-made candy. Her decorations were startling and exquisite, for her entire colour scheme was done in scarlet and white with splashes of scarlet poppies throughout. She invariably arranged the flowers herself, for she was a skilled botanist and had collected and mounted three hundred and sixty-four varieties of wild flowers that grew on the Yukon hills. She was the kind of woman who always made her own place cards and Christmas cards, and she is still doing it today at the age of eighty-five.

Soon after Mrs. Black's arrival in Government House, the national regent of the Imperial Order of the Daughters of the Empire wrote her from Toronto that she would "be pleased if you would select some of the best people in town and form a chapter of the I.O.D.E." This is a patriotic organization similar to the Daughters of the American Revolution. The phrase "best people" amused Mrs. Black, but she sat down and soon had a list worked out. As a result the George M. Dawson chapter of the I.O.D.E. came into being with Mrs. Black as regent. (Dawson was the Government surveyor for whom the town had been named in 1896.)

Years before, in Toronto, I had been asked to join this organization, but being something of a Socialist in those days had refused, for I felt it both snobbish and imperialistic. Now, however, as a staunch Conservative, I was delighted to be included among "the best people". I am afraid that the formation of the chapter caused a great deal of quiet fury among some of the townspeople. For one thing, the Americans could not belong. They hastily got together and formed an American women's club. For another, the merchants' wives were not included. They got together and formed a chapter of their own which, with great diplomacy, they called The Martha Munger Black Chapter (Mrs. Black's maiden name was Martha Munger). I have a feeling, though, that some members of the George M. Dawson chapter persisted in thinking of the Martha Munger Black chapter as the "B" team.

The first big reception of the George M. Dawson chapter was held to celebrate Dominion Day, July 1. For reasons which now escape me, the affair took place, not on the actual day, but on July 3. Government House was ablaze with flags of all nations, with the Union Jack and the Canadian Red Ensign taking prominence. In order to convince the sceptical outside world that Dawson was indeed the land of the midnight sun, we had arranged to have photographs taken of the proceedings on the stroke of twelve o'clock, when it was still quite light, even though the sun had dipped below the hills. During the evening, an incoming steamer whistled and the word went around that the Seattle Chamber of Commerce was aboard and had been invited *en masse* to the reception. We were all quite excited.

The Americans were expected to arrive at Government House about midnight, in time for the picture. The photographer had already set up his cabinet and was waiting for the hour to strike. People in the crowd began to nudge into positions of vantage. Meanwhile, Mrs. Black, who had been born an American, disappeared upstairs, where, it later turned out, she was preparing a surprise for her former countrymen. Across the railing of the upstairs verandah she fastened, crosswise, an enormous Stars and Stripes.

The tourists came, midnight struck, the photographer clicked his shutter. It was only when the guests began to move about again that the giant American flag was to be seen hanging serenely—"brazenly" some said—*above* the dwarfed British flags fluttering on the verandah below. And it was the Fourth of July at that. The following day the photographer developed his pictures and prepared to send them off to the Outside papers and the national headquarters of the I.O.D.E. But the photographs, labelled "Dawson I.O.D.E. Celebrates Dominion Day", showed the group of us dominated by the Stars and Stripes. All the pictures had to be called in while we carefully scissored off the top three inches of each of them.

There always seemed to be some sort of minor storm raging in Dawson on one or another of our various religious, political or fraternal organizations. The political tempests were the most frequent and the most violent. At the political meetings in the A.B. Hall everybody watched everybody else to note the tiniest significant reaction to each speaker. Mrs. Black's gimlet eyes could be seen, in Service's phrase, "rubbering round the room", to note exactly who clapped and who didn't, who smiled at each hoary joke, whose features held an expression of distaste and whose showed approbation.

One needed a poker face at such affairs. "What on earth does she mean, clapping like that?" I heard one Conservative neighbour say of another during the applause for a Liberal speaker. (For both parties would often hold combined meetings.) The day after a rally, every act would be discussed and dissected and the political lines redrawn. "Say, did you see Mrs. Burgess's face when that old Grit windbag was spouting?" a friend said to me at one of these post-mortems. "She couldn't keep the smiles down. And her man with a Government job!"

Inevitably, I found myself caught in the middle of a short-lived political tornado. I went one evening to a Yukon Council election rally with a friend who was pregnant. At the end of the evening, as the hall was close and stuffy and we occupied chairs in the balcony, we decided to leave down the back stairway. I had forgotten that these stairs led directly into the supper-room which served as a general committee room for both parties. It was packed with excited men, all smoking cigars and talking at the top of their voices. We elbowed a pathway through this confusion towards the door, but suddenly found ourselves face to face with Norman Watt, the Liberal candidate. Without thinking, I committed a heinous crime. I not only held out my hand to this monster but also, in a high-pitched voice that carried across the room to the Conservative ranks, I told him that I had enjoyed his speech.

This was bad enough, by all odds, but I later learned that I had added injury to insult by "kicking", "knocking", "stepping on" (there were various versions) the august body of the Conservative candidates, who stood unseen and unacknowledged directly behind me. I was, of course, unconscious of all this until Frank, looking a little shaken, came home for lunch the next day.

The first thing that morning he had had a call from an infuriated Tory organizer who had given a graphic account of the incident and hinted that, if there were to be no repercussions, "Mrs. Berton had better get busy and explain, as best she can, her side of the story to the people at the top." For the sake of peace and quiet, not to mention the job, I did so immediately. I doubt that they quite believed me; after all, I had got my old teaching job under the regime of the hated Liberals.

Into our community, about this time, there entered two quite unlikely people, the nephew of Theodore Roosevelt and his young wife. Gracie Hall Roosevelt (he was Eleanor Roosevelt's brother and F. D. R.'s cousin) was just out of Harvard, twenty-one years of age, tall, rangy, loose-jointed and brimming with ideas. His new bride, Margaret, was a dark, pleasant-faced girl of twenty whose family lived in Boston. Neither had been on their own before, and it had been Hall Roosevelt's idealistic but quite impractical idea to try to live for a year as a common labourer entirely by the sweat of his brow, without recourse to family, friends or private funds. He had chosen Dawson City for this experiment because it seemed suitably romantic and suitably remote from Boston and New York.

The Roosevelts arrived in our midst one day quite unheralded. Hall donned the roughest blue jeans and went to work as a labourer for the power company. (He had an electrical engineering degree from Harvard.) Almost everybody thought he was quite mad. Few believed he was really the nephew of the ex-president of the United States. Dawson drew to its bosom all sorts of strange people claiming impossible claims and I think Hall and Margaret were placed in this category. On his first Sunday in town, I remember, Hall in morning clothes and silk hat called at Government House and left his card. This produced absolutely no reaction. Hall was startled. It wasn't that he was being snubbed; it was simply that nobody paid any attention to him.

Frank and I got to know both the Roosevelts very well during their year in Dawson. In fact, I imagine we knew them better than anybody else. It was obvious to both of us that they were not impostors and we enjoyed their company. We had a small poling boat with an engine that year and we took them on river trips during the summer. I remember that Margaret Roosevelt wore the largest solitaire diamond I had ever seen. It began to embarrass her and she soon had it put away in the bank for the rest of her stay.

Hall's idea of living on his resources broke down almost immediately. His wages would hardly have paid for the constant telegrams he dispatched to Washington and New York. Then Margaret became pregnant and Hall at once sent all the way to Boston for a nurse for her. They lived in a small, nondescript cabin in the unfashionable north end of Dawson—"the wrong side of the tracks", as Margaret kept saying delightedly. A steady stream of parcels kept arriving for them from the United States. Nobody quite knew what to make of all this. "Have you noticed the number of books those new people keep getting in?" Mrs. Coldrick said to me one day. "You know, I think they must have kept a book-store Outside.

It was not a very successful year for the Roosevelts in Dawson. They were lonely most of the time. They didn't move in the social set, for, ironically, they were not quite accepted. They slipped away finally, without any fanfare, but when they got to Seattle they bought an expensive Persian rug which they sent to Frank and me as a present. The customs man in Dawson had never seen one before. He thought it was an "old mat" and made no charge.

It was shortly after this that the First World War fell on Dawson like a bombshell. We had all read skimpy reports of European troubles in the *Dawson Daily News*, but Europe, really, seemed a planet or so away. Then one night during a motion picture, the lights went on, and George Black, telegram in hand, mounted the stage and read the news to us.

Next day several members of the police who were army reservists left by boat on active service, and a few days later The Bird rapped on our door. He had been out of town since spring working a lay on an Eldorado claim.

"I've come to say good-bye," he announced. "Off on the next boat."

"Off?"

"That's what. Can't idle here, y'know. Country needs me."

"Well, it can't last long. You'll soon be back."

"Don't fool yourself. Real thing this time. Serious."

I wished him God-speed with a sinking heart. I never saw him again.

Within a week Joe Boyle, the flamboyant mining king, was

recruiting his own personal machine-gun battery. Boyle had become one of the most controversial figures in town. One point of dispute was the price his power company charged for electricity to the townspeople—forty cents a kilowatt hour. (We didn't pay it: Frank, ever inventive, tinkered with the meter.) Boyle was a doer, not a thinker, and his three great dredges—the biggest in the world—were solidly munching pay gravel from his huge Klondike River concession. Among his many feats, he had dammed the north fork of the Klondike, diverted the entire river so that it ran over paying property, stripping off the top-soil and thawing out the frozen ground so that it could be mined. All the same he always seemed on the verge of bankruptcy and often enough his men had to wait for their money. Yet he was a generous man who liked to do everything in a big, openhanded manner. His old partner, Frank Slavin, the boxer, had gone broke in Vancouver. When Boyle heard of it, he gave Slavin a job in the company in "a roving position" so he could pay him a good salary.

In the early years Boyle had personally managed and financed the Dawson hockey team and sent it on a continent-wide tour through the U.S. and Canada. Now with the war hardly a week old Boyle was personally recruiting men to fight, and paying for their uniforms, weapons and training out of his own pocket, as a present to the Government. He himself became an honorary lieutenant-colonel and promptly designed two collar badges of solid Yukon gold. One dark night in October, the entire town turned out to wave the battery good-bye as the last boat pulled out into the river.

It was a melancholy occasion, as all last boats were, but this one especially so. I can still see them shuffling through the dark (Tom Kirkpatrick, who had come in with me on the stage, was one of them), Boyle in a heavy ulster marching at their head, all of them in civvies because they would have to go through neutral American territory before reaching Vancouver. The I.O.D.E. had given them each a wrist-watch and Charlie Jeanerette of the Klondike Nugget and Jewellery Shop had made pins shaped like miniature gold pans for each of them. Their slogan was "Dawson to Berlin".

They never fought as a unit. They were broken up soon after reaching training camp, but that did not prevent them from fighting and dying gallantly in the mud of the Somme and on the slopes of Vimy. Every officer who left that night and twenty-four of the forty men received decorations. This was a record for any Canadian Army unit in the First World War.

As the boat pulled out they were still cheering from the decks and shouting "Dawson to Berlin". Forty per cent of them never returned. But we could not know that as we waved from the dock. The war still seemed far away and one could not hear the rumble of the guns behind the trembling aspens of the Yukon hills.

It was now George Black's turn to try to organize a force of men, but it took two years of pleading with the Government to release him. In 1916 he was finally given leave of absence from his post as commissioner to raise the Yukon Expeditionary Force. Nobody seemed astonished to find that Mrs. Black was going overseas with him. I don't think I would have been more than mildly surprised to find that she had won a Military Cross in the trenches, but she stopped short of this. The generals were nonplussed when she announced her intention of sailing to Europe on a troopship. "Why," one of them expostulated, "these ships are only for men." Mrs. Black retorted that she had crossed the Chilkoot in the company of several thousand men and hadn't the least objection to crossing the Atlantic with several thousand more. She won her point and in England gave literally hundreds of lectures about the Yukon, all for the benefit of the war effort, and spent her spare hours rolling bandages for the Red Cross while her husband and son were in the fighting lines.

Frank went out with the Black company, but as it was an infantry unit and he was a graduate engineer, he switched to the Royal Canadian Engineers when he reached Vancouver. I went with him. Again, we took the last boat out of town. The ice was already forming along the shore and great lumps were floating sluggishly down the river. The hills around us were brown and dead and there was a smell of snow in the air. The inevitable crowd on the dock, waving from the darkness, seemed smaller than it ever had before. Then the town's lights vanished as we chugged around the bluff. It was five years before we saw Dawson again.

Ten

WHEN the war ended and Frank returned safely we had a major decision to make about our lives. Would we settle Outside, renouncing the Yukon for ever, or would we go back to the dying Klondike? It was a hard decision to make, but in the end the North won. I know that the phrase "the spell of the Yukon" has become a cliché since Robert Service first coined it, but that does not make it any the less powerful. Certainly, we spent long hours discussing plans for settling down in the fruit lands of Ontario or among the roses of Vancouver Island. But we both knew, deep down inside ourselves, that the Yukon was our life and we could not give it up.

There is a phrase in the North which people still use about those who cannot bring themselves to leave. "He's missed too many boats," they will say. Well, I guess Frank and I had missed too many boats. I had only meant to stay in the Yukon one year; he had gone, long before me, to stay just two years. Now we were preparing to go back again for the remainder of our lives.

I think as we talked over our plans that the thoughts of both of us harked back to a certain summer's day almost a decade before, in the early days of our marriage. It comes back to me now as sharply as if it had all happened yesterday. We had struggled for hours up a steep, tangled gulch, our feet deep in wet caribou moss and our legs and ankles bruised by sharp rocks. Then, suddenly, we broke out on to a sunlit hillside. On its upper reaches, fairly dancing with the joy of life, was a grove of young white birches. Lower down, towards the valley, lay acres and acres of wild flowers—clumps of blue lupins, larkspur five feet tall, monkshood and great feathery bunches of white Baby's Breath. We never spoke of that scene to each other again, but it was one of the reasons why we were returning.

But we did not go back immediately to Dawson. Instead, Frank found himself transferred to Whitehorse as Government agent. Here he held the posts of mining recorder, fire warden, inspector of weights and measures and half a dozen other jobs all rolled into one. We arrived, typically enough, on an October day late in 1919 in the midst of a blinding blizzard.

Whitehorse was still the sleepy little town I had first seen twelve years before on my way into the Yukon. Its population still stood at three hundred—three hundred that is before the boat crews and ships' carpenters and those townspeople lucky enough to take a winter holiday had left for the Outside. When the snow came Whitehorse was like a deserted village.

It was a neat, tidy community, in sharp contrast to Dawson, built on volcanic ash and clay. There were few tumbledown or boarded-up shacks, no piles of mining machinery, no weed-choked ditches. It was bordered by the headwaters of the Yukon on one side and a low plateau on the other. We ate plenty of mountain sheep in season, and it was possible to get salad greens all winter each time the coast boat docked in Skagway. The eggs were fresher, and therefore, to Dawsonites, insipid. After the rich orange storage eggs, these tasted quite flat. There was also more sunshine in the winter, for we were three hundred miles farther south. Even on the shortest day we could still see our shadows.

Whitehorse was also a quieter town than Dawson. It was, indeed, a typical northern small town with no metropolitan aspirations. Dawson was in no sense typical of anything—it was unique. Whitehorse was pretty well a company town, for the White Pass and Yukon Transportation Company kept it going. The social climate was not the same as in Dawson and there was bitter rivalry between the citizens of the two towns, as is often the case in neighbouring communities. (In the Yukon three hundred odd miles is still "neighbouring".) Whitehorse felt it was neglected by the Federal Government and claimed Dawson "hogged everything". To Dawsonites, Whitehorse was nothing more than a jumping-off place and they made no secret of their superiority. I must say I got the impression that Dawson people were none too welcome in Whitehorse and certainly in the time we were there we kept pretty much to the Dawson crowd.

Politics was partly responsible for this. Whitehorse was a Liberal town; Dawson was now Conservative. The Blacks, indeed, used to claim that they had to sneak through White-horse from steamboat to train, hiding their faces as they went. This was melodramatic overstatement, for as a matter of fact the Blacks were often tendered a reception and a dinner in Whitehorse. All the same this was the general impression. Political distinctions were so carefully drawn that our friends warned us when we arrived to divide our patronage carefully, when buying provisions, between Capt. Paddy Martin's grocery and general store (Liberal) and Taylor and Drury's emporium (Conservative). Throughout our two years in Whitehorse we systematically dealt with one shop one month and then, in the next month, with the other.

In this atmosphere we were glad to see anybody from Dawson, or, indeed, anyone who was at all familiar. We soon struck up an acquaintance with, of all people, Dolly Orchard, the ex-dance-hall girl, and her husband, Jimmy Turner, who had been the subject of considerable gossip in Dawson. The last we had heard of them she had been taking in miners' washing on the creeks to make ends meet, but now he had a good Government job. Dolly had become a Christian Science healer and was well liked by the townspeople. She still had the same wonderful hair and alluring eyes that had made her the toast of the dance-halls, but no mention was ever made of her gaudy past. It turned out that among other people she had cured my first Yukon escort, Mr. Hamilton, of alcoholism. I had last seen him standing drunkenly on the river bank as our boat pulled away from the shore. Now he was a frequent and sober visitor to the town.

The only connecting link between Whitehorse and the Outside was the little narrow-gauge railway running over the White Pass to Skagway. The train came in twice a week during the winter unless, as seemed perennially the case, it was snow-bound, blocked by a rockslide or a flooded river. When this happened our isolation was complete. There was no fresh milk, for all the cows were in Skagway. There was no mail and usually no telegraph service, for in periods of bad weather the wires were down. There was no undertaker, for he too came from Skagway.

One winter while we were in Whitehorse a trapper was frozen to death outside his cabin several miles downriver. A patrol of police went out to bring in the body. Unfortunately the wretched man had met his death while struggling to open his cabin door. His arms were outstretched and his legs spread-eagled. The undertaker happened to be in town when news of the tragedy came out, so in order to save an extra trip he remained in Whitehorse to prepare the corpse for burial. But when the frozen cadaver was brought in by sleigh he faced a problem: how to bury a spread-eagled corpse in a Christian coffin. The only answer was to wait while the body slowly thawed, a process that took longer than anybody imagined. The impatient undertaker had to miss several trains.

Train day was an event in Whitehorse. It meant mail, fresh milk, green vegetables, strangers in town. And during the summer when one of the semi-weekly steamboats was also in town waiting to take its load to Dawson to connect with the Lower River steamers *en route* to Fairbanks, Alaska, the town really woke up. It was considered no more than a patriotic duty for every true Whitehorse booster to swell the crowd at station or dockside. As one socialite explained to me shortly after my arrival, "I think it's our duty to show the tourists that we're not all Indians and Eskimos and that we know how to dress decently."

In the winter of course it was the Overland Stage that connected with the train. Its facilities had been greatly depleted since I had made my journey to Dawson a decade before. There were fewer travellers to the mining camps now, for the palmy days were over. Many of the road-houses which in the old days had been spotted every twenty-two miles along the winter road were closed. Passengers now had to provide their own lunches and these were eaten in the open after being thawed out by a bonfire on the side of the trail. In the old days we had made the journey in less than a week. Now the stage only made a post a day and, if the trail was bad, the trip often took longer than a fortnight.

This was too long for many men and there were great numbers who preferred to walk to Dawson with their goods on their backs, following the tracks of the stage in the snow. We had not been long in Whitehorse before Arthur Coldrick, the Englishman who had been on the stage when I travelled aboard it, arrived in town from the Outside.

"I'm walking in, you know," he said, talking as casually as if he were about to take a stroll down Regent Street. And off he went, in his brisk way, on a three-hundred-and-sixty-mile hike through deep snow, lonely forest, frozen river and high plateau, in the dead of winter with the thermometer well below zero and the blue Aurora his only beacon. A short time later we had a letter from him from Dawson, describing the experience. He spoke glowingly of the climate and the scenery, but less enthusiastically of the sleeping-quarters, which had certainly degenerated. He told us about one place where all the stage passengers slept in a large stable divided by a canvas-partitioned room in the centre. He said he didn't mind mice rummaging around his feet, but the strong smell of ammonia from the horses made sleep difficult.

We had not been in Whitehorse three months before I

realized that after eight years of marriage I was going to become a mother. After my years of handling other people's children I was to have one of my own. But my satisfaction was leavened by some slight feelings of anxiety. Whitehorse had a much smaller and more primitive hospital, devoid of the facilities of the larger institution in Dawson. The doctors had a habit of flitting in and out of town like bees moving from flower to flower. And I was no longer young. I was forty-two years old, facing my first baby. Nor was I heartened by the fact that the two Dawson kindergarten teachers who had followed me on the staff and had later been married had each died in child-birth at a younger age. I could see my friends looking at me queerly and a little tragically, as if I were already marked for death, and could almost hear them whispering, behind my back, "Will she make the third in a row?"

But my greatest worry, during the months of waiting, was the town doctor. He just wouldn't stay put. I started out with one doctor but he left town within a month or two under tragic circumstances. His wife had died of influenza and the events attendant on her death were particularly grisly. While the poor woman was still alive it had been necessary to summon the undertaker from Skagway to stand by until the end came. Otherwise he would have missed his train again. As a result of this, the doctor had no stomach for Whitehorse and he departed.

Now we were without a doctor and the town's health was entrusted to the care of the druggist's assistant, as the druggist himself was Outside for the winter. I was decidedly dubious about going to him for obstetrical care, for it seemed to me that he had more experience selling picture postcards of Robert Service's cabin than he had in the practice of pharmacology.

It was two months before Doctor No. 2 arrived. He was a fine-looking man and the town liked him. Unfortunately we liked him better than he liked us, for at the end of the month he took himself off and once again we were at the mercy of the drug-store clerk.

My time was drawing near when Doctor No. 3 arrived, heralded by numerous reports as to his ability and experience, not to mention the inevitable details about his background, family, spare-time pursuits and love life, which were all tied up neatly in the verbal parcel of information which preceded every new arrival into the North.

I received my summons on a hot July day when the flies were thick and the dogs lay sleeping in the dust of the main street and the thermometer stood at ninety-two in the shade. I walked briskly to the hospital, showing a boldness I did not feel, accompanied by husband, dog and a thick horde of mosquitoes. The hospital was almost as empty as the grave; the only other occupant was an elderly Indian being treated for a carbuncle.

Now began a curious ordeal. The windows of my room opened on to the main street and as my pains began to increase in regularity and sharpness I became aware of a conversation being carried on by two women standing on the sidewalk below. They were old acquaintances, one an ex-schoolteacher married to a White Pass official, and the other the wife of the principal, a stout, florid Englishwoman of fifty named Mrs. Fortesque, who had a passion for grotesque Victorian hats and a great love for tittle-tattle. She especially loved to go calling, for she clung tenaciously to the social forms which had been drummed into her as a girl in an English cathedral town. She called on all newcomers within two weeks of their arrival in town, and when anyone left town she called again. She called on brides with good wishes, on the sick for speedy recovery, on mourners with deepest sympathy. Immaculately gloved and bearing her antique card-case, with the proper inscription for the proper occasion written in a flowing script in the upper left-hand corner, Mrs. Fortesque was always on hand with congratulations or condolences when fortune smiled or disaster befell. As the pains engulfed me I became aware of the fact that without a doubt Mrs. Fortesque and her friend were discussing my approaching death, and I began to wonder whether they had already sent for the undertaker from Skagway.

Now the whole question of women in the North crossed my mind again, as it had during my lonely hours on Sourdough Gulch. I could not help but think of poor Mabel McIlwaine, who had succeeded me as kindergarten teacher and had died in child-birth. And Mabel Magwood who had followed her. She married John Henry, the shy science master whom I had first met on my trip into the Yukon. He had planned a dream honeymoon in the wilds of Swede Creek, up the Yukon, where they would live in a tent and commune with nature. Alas, it had all been too much for Mabel, and half-way through this idyllic period she had dragged him back to town again, thoroughly fed up with the nomad's life that so many men and so few women in the Yukon enjoyed. She did not trust the land. When she became pregnant she determined to have her child Outside. She went to a proper hospital and there, ironically, she too died of child-birth.

The whole situation made me furiously angry. I decided that come what may I would spite the chattering women on the street corner and live through my labour. My expression became ferocious and I think it quite startled the nurse who now entered. The baby was coming and she was sweating as profusely as I when suddenly a knock came on the door. The nurse swore, rushed to the door and shouted: "Go away! Go away!" In the hallway I could just spy, out of the corner of my eye, that familiar Victorian hat. The nurse returned, looking grim and bearing an engraved calling card on which Mrs. Fortesque had written, in her beautiful script, the words "With kindest enquiries". I am sure she had a second one ready for Frank "With deepest condolences".

A few moments later the doctor arrived and delivered me of a healthy baby boy. But before I was out of hospital, he too had fled the town. I really think the poor man was distressed by the excellent health of the townspeople and departed for sicklier climes. He was replaced sometime later by Doctor No. 4.

We brought the baby up in the kitchen of our bungalow. My mind reverts to it today whenever I see the sleek, modern kitchens which have nothing at all visible but drawers, cupboards and handles. My own kitchen in the north was a sort of G.H.Q., the most important room in the house. It was here that the whole family, dog included, took its weekly Saturday-night bath. It was here that the Monday wash was soaked and wrung out and dried on a complicated arrangement of ropes and pulleys suspended from the ceiling. It was here that the man of the house shaved and here, in the fall, where he brought home the kill from the hunt and butchered it for winter's use. The kitchen was dining-room and den and now, on top of everything else, it became a nursery.

The child's first year was normal enough, enlivened only by occasional hazards peculiar to the Yukon. It was my habit to set him out in the yard on the crisp spring days when there was still plenty of snow on the ground, tying him securely in his pram and giving him a bread crust to gnaw on while I worked in the kitchen. But one day when I did this I was disturbed by a loud cry from him and on going out found the crust gone. I gave him another but in a few moments it had vanished, too, and he was crying again. The crusts continued to disappear as fast as I gave them to him and it was only when I watched from the window that the mystery was solved. Quick as a wink a great Canada jay swooped down, seized the bread from the child's hands and made off with it while he looked on with an expression half of fear, half of interest on his face. In the Yukon the bird is colloquially known as Camp Robber and rightly so. He is the boldest bird I know.

The baby's closest friend, our dog Grey Cloud, looked more like a wolf. This was not surprising, for his grandfather had been a timber wolf. He had a soft, long-haired coat—silver grey with highlights of amber—and a magnificent tail that curved over his back like a graceful willow plume. He had a gentle but tragic expression and there was nothing of the wolf about his temperament. He was a pacifist among dogs, a canine philosopher who enjoyed quiet walks in quiet places and hated the fierce, sudden fights that sprang up like passing squalls in the streets of the town. There always seemed to be one of these dog fights going on, involving several huskies all tearing at each other in a tight ball of fur and teeth. When Grey Cloud sighted one of these brawls he would pretend not to see it, but holding his head high would look intently in front of him until we were well past. He liked nothing better than to accompany the baby and me as I wheeled him through the quiet woods behind our cabin.

These walks in midsummer were often marred by the presence of mosquitoes and black flies, which were far worse in Whitehorse than in Dawson. It is almost impossible to describe to those who have not experienced it the fearful ordeal of walking through these swarms of insects that, in the early days, quite literally drove unprepared men insane. During the height of the fly season we simply could not venture outside the house without wearing a thick head-dress of black chiffon which covered our heads and came down tight around our shoulders. Without this, existence out of doors was pure and simple hell. In addition it was important to wear gloves and heavy stockings so that every possible square inch of bare flesh was covered. Before our days at Whitehorse came to an end we believed the story of the mosquitoes which attacked a man carrying home a copper wash-boiler. Unable to cope with them, he took refuge inside the boiler, only to find that they were stinging him right through it. Desperately he seized a rock and hammered each stinger as it came through the metal. At this the insects rose up in a cloud and, finding themselves securely fastened down, flew away taking the boiler with them.

Before we left Whitehorse and were recalled to Dawson, the first aeroplane flew into the North and landed on a plateau above the town. The entire village flocked up the hill to look at the strange machine, which seemed to be all wire and struts. Nobody could know then that the aeroplane would be the making of Whitehorse, that this wild, wooded plateau would one day become the biggest airfield in the North, that the sky over the town would become black with 'planes and that, while Dawson slowly shrank on the banks of the Klondike, Whitehorse would rise to a wartime population of thirty thousand men, building the Alaska Highway and Canol pipe-line system and manning the North-West Staging Route to Alaska. Whitehorse's day was yet to come, but that day was still a long way off. When we left it, the town was still a thin line of frame buildings acting as a stepping-stone between the Outside world and the Klondike.

Eleven

AFTER two years in Whitehorse, the Government recalled Frank to the Dawson mining recorder's office and we returned again to the town that each of us now thought of as home. We bought another furnished house with a garden full of vegetables (for we had long since sold our pre-war home) and settled down. The house was of a pattern with Dawson's frame buildings, a five-room bungalow with wide verandahs, double walls insulated against the cold with a foot of sawdust filling, and foundations that continually heaved and swayed in the frost-racked ground. We were on Eighth Avenue again, under the hill, directly across the dusty road from Robert Service's little shrine of a cabin.

At first glance Dawson looked exactly as it had on the day I first saw it from the decks of the riverboat—the same grey-roofed buildings, the same helter-skelter of cabins. But on second glance there was no doubt at all that we were living in a decaying town. The population had now sunk to eight hundred, though there were buildings enough for ten times that number. Dozens more houses were standing empty, dozens more lots were vacant, dozens more buildings were slowly falling to pieces. Ninth Avenue, on the upper edge of town, had vanished into the encroaching bush and weeds. Eighth Avenue, where we now lived, was almost empty of people. The north end of town had become a desert of boarded-up cabins. For Dawson had shrunk in towards its core. Of West Dawson, that once-lively community across the Yukon River, scarcely a vestige remained. Klondike City was empty and dead, its only inhabitant a respectable mulatto woman named Ida Mason, who, for all the years I knew her, wore a jacket and white whipcord breeches on her journeys into town.

What a contrast this ill-famed suburb now presented, compared with its heyday! The hotel from which the white-coated waiters had once carried trays of beer to the prostitutes stood at a drunken slant, closed up. The busy sawmill was shut for ever. Of the brewery, which had once done a roaring business, nothing whatever remained. The railway, which had run from here to the mines, no longer operated and the cars stood out to pasture, the tracks long since rusted and covered with weeds. The neat little rows of two-roomed cabins which had seen, beneath the northern lights, so many strange sights, were now all empty, the names of their former occupants only faintly visible on the doors.

In Dawson itself, life had slipped a gear or two. Many of my old friends were gone. The teachers were all new. Mr. Bragg had left. There were new policemen, new doctors, new nurses, new clergymen. Even Diamond Tooth Gertie had gone. Her husband had been burned to death in one of Dawson's frequent fires. The *Dawson Daily News* was now issued thrice weekly and we were down to one theatre and three churches—the Christian Scientists and Methodists had both given up the good fight. We were down to one hospital, the Roman Catholic; the Good Samaritan had been disbanded and its building was now used as a Church of England hostel for half-breed children who came out of the woods to attend school each winter.

If many of the buildings were empty, the hospital was full, not of patients, but of old men. The Government paid the keep of these indigent sourdoughs who could no longer care for themselves. All had come over the trail in '96 and '97 and '98 and now they could be seen sitting on the verandah in the sun staring out at the river which had brought them here. We used to organize concert parties for them and I grew to know some of them quite well. Many had gone crazy in their cabins. I remember one old man who sat in his chair on the verandah in the belief that he was travelling up the river on a steamboat.

"I think we're reaching Stewart City, now, aren't we, nurse?" he kept saying, and the nurse would nod and say that Stewart was just around the corner.

My kindergarten was closed now and its premises were occupied by the library, for the former library building, along with dozens of others, had burned down in the intervening years. Most of the children I had taught were still in town, grown now to adulthood. Many of them had not yet been outside of Dawson.

Dawson was still a city of hotels, but many of them were empty. The Dawson City Hotel had closed, and the Klondike, and the Green Tree, where Babe Mitchell, the dance-hall girl, was shot, and Belinda Mulroney's famous Fairview. The passing of the Fairview, where men and women in evening dress ate eight-course meals while a five-piece orchestra played, certainly meant the end of an era in Dawson.

And Government House was closed, too, for ever. The office of the commissioner was abolished and George Black, back from the wars, was now the town's leading lawyer and Member of Parliament for the Yukon. His former mansion stood boarded up like the cabins and hotels on Front Street. Within, there was still kept the silver plate and the fine china, the mahogany furniture and the gold wallpaper. All these were carefully maintained against the day when Dawson might boom again. As far as I know, they are still there.

Those people who were left in the town had by this time taken on some of the qualities of Dawson's ageing buildings. When I had first arrived, the men on the dock and those working away on the creeks had all seemed young and vigorous. Now they were growing old and grey. It was a quarter of a century since the rush, and the men who had breasted the passes in their twenties and thirties were now in their fifties and sixties. Many of them looked older, for they had led hard lives.

The war and the passage of time had hit the town heavily, but a greater tragedy had decimated it. In mid-October, 1918, the last boats had left the town as usual, bearing close to three hundred and fifty northerners Outside. In Skagway, these people had boarded the Canadian Pacific Steamship *Princess Sophia*. Two days later the ship went to the bottom of the Lynn Canal, carrying with it every soul on board.

No one, except for the inevitable dog, survived this terrible tragedy—the worst the West Coast has ever seen. The disaster struck the town a blow from which it never quite recovered. One hundred and twenty-five Dawsonites had been wiped out with this single stroke. There was hardly a family that was not hit in some way. The Yukon Gold Company, the Northern Commercial, the Government service, the steamboats, all were shattered by the wreck of the *Sophia*. The crews of twelve river steamers, including three captains, went down with her. The unhealed scars were still on Dawson when we returned to live there.

The bitterness of the *Sophia* tragedy was accentuated by the fact that her entire crew and passenger list could have been saved. The ship left Skagway, bound for Vancouver, on Wednesday, October 23. On Thursday morning, in a blinding snowstorm, she struck a reef and settled there in no great apparent danger. Several vessels rushed to her aid and stood by the foundering ship during the day while their masters begged the captain to debark his passengers. He refused, preferring to wait for another of his own company's ships to come to the rescue. On Friday morning the *Sophia* was still resting on an even keel and again the captain was entreated to debark his passengers. Again he refused. By afternoon, the heavy seas had forced the attendant vessels to seek shelter. The end was swift. By five o'clock, crackling across the ether came a single sentence from the *Sophia's* wireless operator: "Good-bye—we are foundering!" The great ship slid quietly off the reef and into deep water with scarcely any warning, carrying passengers and crew to their deaths.

We had known almost everybody on the *Sophia*. Indeed, her passenger list had been a faithful cross-section of Dawson's polyglot population. It contained old timers, prospectors, socialites, merchants, hotelmen and cheechakos (the colloquial word for tenderfoot).

There was Billy O'Brien, one of the best-known men in the town, a leading Liberal and a ubiquitous baritone, whose presence was in demand at every concert. It was for him that I was to have played at the Liberal meeting that John Black warned me against, fifteen years before. He had five children and two of them attended my kindergarten. After thirteen years he had decided to take his family Outside so the children could see their grandparents. The entire family was wiped out on the *Sophia*.

There was John Helliwinkle, one of those strange, gypsylike men whom the Klondike attracted in '98. In the old days he had been a sailor before the mast. In Dawson he failed to find gold, so he became instead a real-estate crank. With an optimism which was so typical of the town he began to buy up real estate in the firm belief that the Klondike would boom again and he would make a killing. He devoted all his energies to it and by the time he was ready to leave for a winter Outside he had fifty-five houses and lots. His cabins are still in Dawson, crumbling away.

There was Sam Henry, a pioneer from the pre-gold rush era, who kept a small grocery store near us. He came to the Yukon in 1896, before gold was discovered, and was a sourdough long before the first rush of crudely built boats swept around the mouth of the Klondike. Sam was a former street-car conductor and he had done moderately well in the Yukon. He had not seen the outside world for twenty-two years, and in the fall of 1918 he decided to leave the Yukon for good. He sold his house and all his furniture, but the idea of quitting the country for ever was too much for him, and at the last moment he re-established his ties with the Klondike by buying all his goods back again. Sam had missed too many boats. It was his tragedy that he caught the *Sophia*.

There was Murray Eads, the owner of the Royal Alexandra Hotel, the man who had ordered the huge nude painting to be packed in over the trail. His whole career had been tied to Dawson's gaudy dance-hall period. He had run the famous old Standard and the Monte Carlo in the days when Alexander Pantages, who later became a theatre magnate, and Tex Rickard, who later became a famous fight promoter, were tending bar. Finally he bought the Exchange which became the Flora Dora and later the Royal Alex. Now he and his wife were gone with their era.

There were Walter Harper and his wife. His father, as much as any man, had left his imprint on the Yukon. Fred Harper had come out from County Antrim, Ireland, in 1873, and thus became one of the first white men in the Yukon. He had prospected and traded up and down the river until Carmack's strike. Then he and Joe Ladue had laid out the streets and avenues of a new town on the frozen delta and named it Dawson City. It was ironic that the name of Harper, which had been tied to Dawson's glory, should also make its appearance among the victims of its tragedy.

There was William Scouse, a Scots coal miner who had worked his way from Pennsylvania to Nanaimo, B.C., when the Klondike called him north. It was he who took the first bucket of rich pay dirt from the richest creek in the world. He owned Number Fifteen on Eldorado, one of the most famous claims in the Yukon, and after he grew wealthy he was in the habit of spending his winters in Seattle and his summers on his properties. He was on his way to Seattle when the *Sophia* went down, and now his cabin on Dago Hill was empty.

There was Walter Barnes, an old prospector from Lovat Gulch on the Klondike. He had an old white horse named Billy who was too feeble to work. Billy, in his day, had hauled more than half a million dollars from the tunnel into the gulch and Barnes was so fond of him that he decided to take him Outside to retire as a reward for his work. Now Walter Barnes and Billy and 340 odd others were drowned with the *Sophia*. Their empty cabins and houses stood about the town like monuments. There was one not far from us. It had been owned by

Edmund Ironsides, the collector of customs for Dawson. He used to write poems, I remember, in the Service tradition and in the summer he kept one of the finest gardens in town. It came as a shock to see his house again, boarded up, with the little garden a tangle of weeds and brown dry grass. He and his mother had both gone down on the *Sophia*. Strangely enough the day before he sailed Ironsides had walked into a Skagway insurance office and bought a thirty-thousand-dollar policy.

The war, too, had taken its toll. My old friend The Bird had been killed in action. He was a sniper. I had a few letters from him, written in his abrupt style—then silence. I never heard the details of his death. Fred Chute, the dreamy, pipe-smoking Englishman who had a title but tried to keep it a secret, was dead, too. His end was typical enough—he had been struck down by a motor-cycle as he walked in an English lane, smoking his pipe and staring up at the clouds. And the two young men we had met up Bonanza Creek, who had been so embarrassed by their bare feet, had both been killed.

And Joe Boyle was gone. Of all the men of the Yukon Machine Gun Battery who had left town that dark wet October night on the last boat, none had gone through a more fantastic series of experiences and adventures than he. The stories about his exploits in Russia and Rumania filtered back to Dawson over the years until he became a legend in the North, as he already was in Europe. Few people believed them then, not even his own brother in Woodstock, Ontario, until one day a foreign-looking couple arrived at the family home with a message from Queen Marie herself, praising him as the saviour of Rumania.

Boyle, separated from his battery, had cooled his heels until 1917, when he was dispatched to Russia as a member of the British Railway Mission. He reached Russia on the eve of the Revolution, and from this moment on his life became a series of bizarre adventures. He moved through the turmoil of the revolutionary Soviet, dodging bullets, knives, fists and cannon, an unkillable giant with his glittering nugget badges and the single word YUKON stitched in black thread on his shoulders. He feuded with the Grand Duke Alexander, fought bare-fisted with a mob on the steps of the Czar's palace, lunched with Kerensky, and was given a safe-conduct pass through the country by Lenin himself.

He led a force of men to the Ploesti oilfields of Rumania, destroying the refining equipment under the noses and machine-guns of the advancing Germans, and he spirited the crown jewels and cash reserves of Rumania out of Russia aboard a stolen railway train. They called him the Uncrowned King of Rumania, and with good reason, for he helped stop the Rumanian revolution, saved the royal couple from assassination, rescued the Grand Duchess Marie from Odessa and plucked a boatload of Rumanian prisoners out of Russian hands. He became the darling of the Rumanian court, to whom he recited the poems of Robert Service, the leading national hero of the country, and the confidant and intimate of the queen, whose lover he was popularly supposed to be. He piled deed upon deed, slipping back time and again into the Soviet until he was the only British subject at large in the land. He prowled through the Black Sea ports disguised as a *muzhik* and escaped from Kiev aboard a death cart crammed with typhoid-fever corpses. He quite literally ran Rumania from behind the throne, and yet he died a forgotten and penniless man in England. During the war his company in the Klondike, which he neglected, ran into financial difficulties. One of his huge dredges sank, causing a staggering loss. His power plant burned to the ground. A legion of creditors won judgments against him. Boyle, suddenly grown as old and shrunken as Dawson itself, dragged himself away like a wounded animal to a lonely lair where he died almost alone, fearful to the last that some of his friends might see him as an old man, and not as the robust soldier of fortune whose exploits had won him seven foreign decorations, as well as the British D.S.O. and O.B.E. Now, on the Klondike, his company was being swallowed up in Arthur Treadgold's dream of one great company, and his dredges were becoming part of the

Yukon Consolidated Gold Corporation, which was rapidly coming to control the entire Klondike.

In Dawson, shrunken by war and disaster and old age, the pre-war pattern of social life went on, though on a smaller scale. The engraved calling cards still piled up in little mounds in the silver salvers, and the eight-course dinners with candlelight and wine still continued behind the log and frame walls. Everybody clung to her "day" for calling, and bridge parties were so lavish that one of my own took two consecutive evenings.

But the social lines had blurred slightly as the population shrunk. There was only one chapter of the I.O.D.E. and everybody belonged to it, whether they were, in the words of the national regent, "the best people" or not. The Mounted Police constables were now more or less accepted at the dances and in the homes of the townspeople and a new phrase "scarlet fever" was brought into use to describe the malady of any girl who had a Mountie for a beau. (I remember one prominent lawyer's daughter who married a policeman. Her mother refused to send notices of the wedding to her friends Outside because he was only a sergeant.) At the formal balls in the A.B. Hall the Grand March was no longer led by the town's elite, but by anybody who happened to get in line first. And the female teachers now lived alone, without stigma.

Dawson had, in fact, become one big family. Everyone knew everyone else. When we passed anybody on the streets we said "hello" because we always knew him. When we called anybody on the phone we did not give a number. We simply said, "Get me Mrs. Macauley, will you, Jean?" The downtown people doubled up on jobs which were no longer sufficient to keep one man fully employed. The secondhand-furniture man was also the undertaker. This was a particularly apt division of work, for Dawson had plenty of used furniture and plenty of graves.

It was now almost impossible to get help and when we went to one of the year's big affairs we took our babies with us. They slept silently in their sleighs in the big dressing-room at the end of the hall. If one came in late and threw one's coat casually over the mountain of furs in the room, she was often startled to hear a tiny cry coming from beneath the mound of clothing. The older children ran about on the curtained stage at the far end of the hall, or threaded in between the dancers on the floor. By early morning they could all be found asleep in the boxes that ran along the gallery.

And we still danced the minuet. It was easily the most popular number of the evening, though it was a little pathetic now to watch it in progress. When the orchestra struck up the familiar strains everybody in the hall, no matter how old or fat or tired, stood up and executed the delicate steps. I can still see the lined faces of the old men lighting up when the minuet was played, for it was their link with a golden youth. The music is no longer familiar to a generation reared on juke-box jingles, but when I hear it today, my mind goes back to the Arctic Brotherhood Hall in Dawson City and that incongruous spectacle of the sourdoughs gamely pirouetting and bowing as the snow swept down outside and the huskies howled to each other across the empty cabins.

Twelve

I WAS no longer a member of the young crowd, nor could I be said to be one of "the crowd who went out" in Dawson. I was a mother, and being a mother in the Klondike could be an exacting business. Shortly after returning to the town I again confounded the pessimists by bearing a healthy eight-pound girl in St. Mary's Hospital. I was now forty-three years old.

The hospital was modern enough and the sisters skilled and patient, but it faced hazards that plagued every institution in Dawson in those days: it had difficulty attracting competent help. As a result my baby almost died in her first week. My suspicions were aroused when the child suddenly dropped off to sleep after a crying spell. Her only attendant was a German assistant who had never taken nurse's training. I finally got the regular nurse, who found it impossible to waken the baby. By now a strange rattling in the child's throat signalled the alarm. The doctor was called post-haste and he immediately ordered hot bottles. Early next morning he brought her round, but it had been a close thing. The German woman had given the baby a hefty dose of soothing syrup and it had been the death rattle that I had heard in her throat. I still shiver when I think of that night.

The baby was baptized by Bishop Stringer, who was back in Dawson after a wartime sojourn in England, where he had caused a sensation. "He has the forehead of a doctor of divinity, the physique and jaw of a prizefighter and the mild blue eyes of a child," one London newspaper eulogized. He and Mrs. Stringer had dined with the King and Queen by royal command. Now he was back in his diocese, where the people, meeting him on the street, were in the habit of saying, "My God, Bish, it's good to see you back!" The bishop was still crossing the Fort McPherson Divide regularly, but now his wife went along with him. It turned out that, after all these years, he had a weak heart and it was her scheme to keep him slowed down by pretending herself to be tired. Off they went over the mountains, following no trail or road, clambering over rocks and niggerheads, shooting caribou for food on the way, with a string of dogs carrying their gear, and old Chief Kikwichik of the Peel Indians carrying Mrs. Stringer on his back across the rough mountain streams.

The Blacks were back in town too. They had also met the royal family, and Mrs. Black had been made a Fellow of the Royal Geographical Society for her work collecting Yukon wild flowers. Every fall the two of them vanished into the wilds on a hunting expedition and returned laden with game.

I settled down to keeping a house that, apart from electricity, had no modern conveniences. Our water, for instance, was delivered during the winter months by two men on a cart, four times a week. It was the arrival of the waterman—he was a neighbour and close friend—that was the first sign to the sleeping household that another day had dawned. He and his partner came in the darkness of the early winter mornings, a great cold blast of air sweeping through the house as the double doors of the kitchen swung open. Then the two of them would trudge in, their clothes caked with snow and ice, their moustaches icicled, bearing two wire-handled petrol tins full of water, which they hoisted and slopped into a tank in the corner. A great deal of the water spilled over on to the floor, where it almost instantly froze into a thin sheet, so that when we rose we were faced with a miniature skating rink in our kitchen. On wash days we left out extra containers—pails, jugs, pots, tins—anything that would hold the precious water. It cost us twenty-five cents a bucket and as a result I still catch myself hoarding half jugs of water and debating whether I should save them for future use.

To add to the confusion, our limited kitchen floor space was broken by a trap-door leading down to an underground world almost as important and even more crowded than the house proper. Here was the vegetable room, filled to bursting-point each August with the winter's supply of produce from our garden. Here the vegetables were kept just above freezing-point by a careful adjustment of ventilators invented by Frank, one set opening into the furnace room, the other out of doors. Also in the basement was the furnace, as many cords of wood as could be crammed in, Frank's carpentry bench, and the family cloakroom. Because of the difficulties brought on by the extreme cold it was feasible to service only those buildings on the main streets with sewers and running water during the winter, and as a result we were visited each week by a scavenger's cart, which arrived in the dead of night with much creaking and rattling and disposed of our garbage and offal.

Sometimes I wonder how children ever grew up at all in Dawson, especially with all the present-day hullabaloo about milk, homogenized, pasteurized, vitaminized, raw and whole. In Dawson there was only one dairy, though I never heard it called that. It was run by a Miss Munro, a wan, pioneer woman who kept a few cows, rarely if ever inspected, which she housed in a shed at Guggieville on the Klondike. She was a hard-working woman of great poverty, for cows were difficult to maintain that far north. I never saw her wear any other clothes than the voluminous black dress which over the years turned a dull nondescript grey. Nor do I ever remember seeing her when she did not look worn out. One morning the milk arrived late and Miss Munro apologized, explained that her house and shed had been immersed in the spring floods. She had had to stand all night up to her hips in water in order to keep a calf on a kitchen table and save it from drowning.

Miss Munro delivered the milk three times a week in old whisky bottles stoppered with ancient corks tied in place with pieces of string. The price was twenty-five cents a bottle. I am afraid she never had the time nor the energy, let alone the equipment, to keep these bottles properly clean. I was shocked by this at first and used to try to boil the corks each day, as well as the bottles, but in the end I found it simpler to trust in the Lord and the good clean Yukon air.

There was another old man up Hunker Creek called Irish Tom, who used to bring goat's milk around in an old cart. He had kept goats on Hunker since 1898. One day he stopped at the house, hobbled his horse and, with his stick in one hand and a beer bottle full of goat's milk gripped tightly in the other, presented me with the sample for which he refused payment.

"Sure and it'll be fine for the youngsters, Matham," he said. "For there's nothin' to beat goat's milk."

I thanked him as best I could, trying to conceal my horror at the thick black sediment of dirt at the bottom of the bottle. I felt there surely must have been some accident, so I ordered regular delivery, only to discover that every bottle was the same. Irish Tom simply wasn't conscious of germs. I called off the deal with the best grace possible.

For years I attempted, in an amateurish way, to pasteurize all our milk, but I doubt if I was very successful. In the end, when several children in town came down with glandular trouble traced to the cows in the neighbourhood, we switched to dried and condensed milk. For several years the children didn't taste the fresh variety.

Even more of an ordeal than de-germing the milk was the effort of trying to extract a teaspoonful of fresh, or I should say fluid, beef juice from a piece of old, frozen meat that had been brought into the country the previous summer. This was a nerve-racking process. Our refrigerator was an outdoor cupboard whose temperature might register sixty below zero. In order that the frozen steak should not thaw out too soon, which would render it a useless mass surrounded by a plateful of chilly, reddish water, I had to time its arrival in the hot kitchen with mathematical precision. When the meat was soft, but not runny, I began to toast it on the end of a fork. This was supposed to kill any germs that had survived the ice. As we used wood for cooking, the fire was either so hot that the entire piece was charred or so nearly out that it was merely smoked.

After the searing was accomplished, successful or not, I would slash the meat with a sharp knife and place it in a metal contraption with a hand crank not unlike an old-fashioned lemon-squeezer. How much juice resulted from this operation depended on two factors: the strength and stamina of my forearm and the original life stream of the animal. If I got a teaspoonful I considered myself lucky.

As for green foodstuffs, we had them in abundance in summer and fall and hardly at all in winter. After Christmas we had to depend pretty well on bottled spinach and wait until the first boat arrived at the end of May. Except for berries, which we froze ourselves—blueberries, raspberries, cranberries and currants—our only fruit was apples and oranges, and even these gave out long before spring. As for salad greens, there weren't any all winter.

I have reason to remember the orange shortage because it was in May at the end of that second post-war winter in Dawson that our small boy came down with pneumonia. He became delirious and parched with fever, crying continually for orange juice. There wasn't an orange for sale in town, and though his cries echoed down the hospital corridors we were powerless to do anything. Succour came from an unexpected quarter. In the next room a middle-aged prostitute lay critically ill. Through those telephone walls she heard the baby's cries, and when told about the dearth of oranges, sent him some from her private supply. The cries stopped and we were thankful. I was less broad-minded in those days than I am now and to my eternal shame I could not bring myself to go in and thank her. This I have always bitterly regretted.

With the coming of the first boat we had fresh fruit again, but oranges still retailed at a dollar and a half a dozen. Prices were always high in Dawson, the result mainly of the heavy freight rates and the seasonal shortages. There were no coins in town smaller than a twenty-five-cent piece and "two bits" was as common a word to us as *"mañana"* is to a Chilean. A newspaper was two bits. So was a bottle of soda pop. A package of needles, a loaf of bread, a beer bottle full of milk—all were two bits. (A beer bottle full of beer was fifty or seventy-five cents.) Motion Pictures, dances and concerts were each a dollar, a price which seemed reasonable then and doesn't seem too unreasonable now. Funerals were the one entertainment that was free.

Indeed, as the years wore on, it was the funerals around which the town revolved. Each cortège, winding slowly up the A.C. Trail, seemed to draw us more tightly together. One was scarcely ended before we were all looking about wondering, not without a certain anticipation, whose would be next. The conventional social bars were dropped at these funerals. We enjoyed our common sorrow to the full and with great democracy. "Oh, Mrs. Berton," one tear-choked washerwoman sniffled as we walked with the crowd from the graveside of a well-known townsman, "wasn't it a *beautiful* funeral!" There were so many funerals now. In my first years in Dawson I could remember very few. Now hardly a week passed without a cortège winding up the trail to the cemetery on the hill.

They soon attained a ritual from which it was impossible to stray. Each funeral must be correct to the smallest detail. The ceremony was almost always held in one of the churches, as the funeral parlour behind the furniture store was inadequate. The edifice was invariably packed and the standing-room-only warning passed around in awestruck and pleased whispers long before the mourners and casket arrived. The sorrowing friends were never allowed to seat themselves casually but were carefully arranged by well-trained ushers at a distance from the central scene carefully calculated in direct ratio to their relative importance either to the community or to the deceased.

In every instance there was an elaborate funeral oration paying tribute to the corpse's fine qualities. We had, I remember, one clergyman, an Englishman of the old-school-tie type, who was new to our ways and ignorant of our customs. He almost made a *faux pas* when, calling upon the disconsolate widow and inquiring as to her wishes regarding hymns, he discovered for the first time that he was expected to deliver a sermon about the deceased.

"But my good woman," he expostulated (for he knew her husband had never entered a church), "there is simply no mention of such a sermon in the Church of England burial service. It—it——" (he stuttered a little) "I mean it simply isn't done—not unless it's for a jolly k-k-ing or something."

At this point the widow broke in dramatically: "You say for a king, yah? Well, I tell *you* my Bill he wass a king. He wass *my* king, you bet. I want you should give him a nize sermon."

Faced with such logic and forced to the wall by the relentless wave of community pressure, the minister gave in and delivered a suitable eulogy.

I suppose the most famous funeral in Dawson occurred on the bright June day when they buried Carl Hafsted. It was the only funeral I know of that did not follow the prescribed pattern, and of all the Dawson funerals it was the only one that now seems to me to have been really cheerful.

Carl Hafsted was a prospector from Quartz Creek and his last wish, before he died, was that his coffin be carried to the top of Haystack Mountain, some distance from Dawson, and buried there, thirty-five hundred feet above sea level.

Hafsted truly loved that mountain and spent the best years of his life in its vicinity. He had it on his mind long before the end, eyeing it wistfully at the end of a long day on his claim, a symbol perhaps of freedom, soaring high above the surrounding country. He knew the request was a difficult one to carry out, for it was no easy task to hoist a heavy coffin up sheer cliffs, so in order to cheer his friends on their way and make the occasion a jolly one—for he said he wanted a happy funeral—he left enough funds to provide a barrel of beer for the mourners.

His instructions were followed implicitly. There was a simple service in a road-house, read by a fellow miner, then off went that strange cortege of thirty men bearing a coffin and a barrel full of beer. It was a weary twelve-mile journey and the party soon had to abandon the wagons and strike off into the bush, felling trees as they went and removing deadfalls and struggling through miles of moss and rocky hillside to get to the base of the mountain. Then, with a thousand feet of sheer climbing left, they rested at midnight and in the bright June light drank Carl Hafsted's beer. The setting was pleasant enough: the rays of the setting sun glinting on the peaks of the Rockies and tinting their snowy tops with gold, the twisted creek running like a silver ribbon through the green shaded valley below.

The climb began again, and the last tough pull to the top took place. Half the party went ahead and sat down on the rocks and braced their feet and pulled on the ropes hitched to the coffin, while those below hoisted it on their shoulders and walked up. Already an advance party had reached the summit, raised a flag and hewn a grave out of the solid rock of the peak. It was four-thirty in the morning in bright sunlight when they laid Carl Hafsted to rest. On top of the grave they sprinkled wild flowers. Then they laid down the pick and shovel he had mined with and the gun he had hunted with, and there, to this day, Carl Hafsted rests in a grave which looks out over the peaks of the Rockies, and the hills where he hunted for moose, and the creeks where he searched for gold.

It was during the winter funerals that the art of Turner Townsend, florist and school janitor, reached its zenith. I never forgot my first Dawson funeral when, looking up from my place in the choir, I beheld, in the dead of Arctic winter, a riot of flowers—on the altar, on the chancel steps and overflowing into the aisles. There were flowers of every shape and variety worked into crosses, anchors, wreaths and sprays. It was a moment or two before I realized they were all artificial.

There were wreaths of gay daisies and marigolds and lush-looking French roses. There were crosses of poppies, lilies of the valley and sweet peas, occasionally garnished by a sprig of fresh green leaves from a local wandering Jew plant. If Turner

Townsend ran short before the winter's end, he ransacked the town's hat shops. Thus, in spite of sub-zero weather, friends could send a floral tribute to the departed. It made for a beautiful funeral and sounded well in the paper next day. It was only when the dyes faded with the snows and the relentless winds plucked at the wreaths that the dried old pieces of cloth sticking to the grave mounds in the cemetery took on a grisly appearance. By spring the graveyard presented a drab and strangely depressing sight, with its faded, torn nosegays blown helter-skelter about. It was somehow like Dawson itself, an artificial city once gay and bright as a spring flower, now faded and desolate, a great graveyard on the banks of the Klondike.

Thirteen

THE Yukon is the coldest and deadliest river that I know, a slate-grey watercourse slipping majestically for twenty-two hundred miles from its headquarters in northern British Columbia to its mouth at the Bering Sea. In places it is so narrow that a boat can hardly slip through its rocky walls. In other sections it is so vast that a man can lose himself for a lifetime in its hundreds of channels. Its banks are sometimes so high that they tower over a three-storey river steamer, but in many places there are no banks at all and the river slops over the surrounding countryside for miles. It rushes at an express-train pace over the rocks of swift rapids and meanders leisurely through the moose pastures of northern Alaska. In the summer its channel is thick with caribou, its little soughs black with ducks, its bars speckled with sandpiper, plover and snipe, its sandy banks pocked with swallows' nests. In the winter it is a rough washboard of ice blocks, thick with snow. It is the life stream of the North, the great aorta down which men and ore and ships and animals come and go; without it the country could hardly have been settled at all. But it is a death stream as well. It is said that if a man falls into the Yukon he will never come out, and for hundreds of men this has been true. The bitter water chills to the marrow, the nests of whirlpools drag the unwary under. A stick thrown into the water will vanish at once, sucked to the bottom by the undercurrent. For all of its length, back and forth across the Arctic Circle, from Lake Bennett to St. Michael, the Yukon hisses and boils continually, a witch-watercourse that the Indians named "greatest river".

In 1924 Dawson's best-known physician, Dr. Lachapelle, vanished into the Yukon River. He was a pioneer of the gold-rush days who had practised for almost thirty years in the town. He was a lover of the river and each September when the ducks were winging south he took to his canoe with his little brown cocker spaniel, Rufus, and took off after game. This September he centred around the mouth of the Stewart, where the Yukon breaks into sloughs and islands, and duckponds and moose licks are plentiful. Two weeks later he loaded his canoe with a bag of ducks and geese and headed back for Dawson, seventy miles away. The last man to see him alive was the road-house keeper at Stewart City, who waved him good-bye. But in Dawson that same afternoon an eerie thing occurred. The doctor's Japanese housekeeper heard the kitchen door open and, looking up, saw her master standing in the doorway, his clothes dripping with water. As she rose to greet him the apparition faded and she ran screaming to the neighbours, who scoffed at the whole story. A week later, when a police patrol found the doctor's canoe with a hole in the bottom and the footprints of a small dog on a wet sandbar, we all had reason to recall that bizarre vision. The body was never recovered but several weeks later a bedraggled and half-starved spaniel made his way back to the Stewart City road-house. The little dog hung around Dawson for years afterwards, a reminder of the tragedy on the river.

In the fall of 1925 and early summer of 1926 we ourselves experienced the Yukon River. We went by steamer in the fall and we came back by poling boat the following spring. By the time we returned to Dawson we knew every twist and turn of the four hundred odd miles of channel between Whitehorse and the Klondike.

I had decided to take the children out to eastern Canada to see their grandparents. Frank could not take the time off, but he agreed to meet us in Whitehorse the following June for a leisurely trip down the river. He stood on the dock, one mid-August day, a lonely figure, waving to us as the steamer *Casca* chuffed slowly around the bend.

The boat trip down from Whitehorse to Dawson seldom took more than thirty-six hours but this upriver journey was a different story. It took four to six days against the stiff current, but it never lacked interest. Norman "Kid" Marion, the pilot on the *Casca*, who had been twenty-five years on the river, told me he never grew tired of it.

"Too much going on, especially coming downstream," he said. "Sands shifting all the time, river changing about . . . new channels, new islands. Always something. Can't tell what you'll run into next. She's treacherous, you know."

Marion was one of the greatest characters of the river. He came from Regina, where, in 1897, he tried to join a detachment of Mounties leaving for Dawson. They rejected him because he was too young. He got a job helping to train dogs for the trail and came to Vancouver with an official party in charge of a group of Cree Indians who were booked to handle the dogs in the North. The Crees quit in Vancouver because the weather was too warm and Marion, who was half Cree himself, was given the job of looking after the dogs. He was the only one who could speak the language to them.

Marion was called "Kid" because he was in his teens when he reached the Klondike. There were men in the Yukon in their sixties still known as "Kid", and Marion bore this nickname until he died. It was reinforced because he had a habit of kidding the tourists. "I used to tell them the truth, but the cheechakos wouldn't believe it," Marion would say. "They're much happier now that I tell 'em lies."

He was a big man with narrow, sleepy eyes, swarthy but with very little trace of his Indian blood. He spoke with a nasal drawl in such a flat, convincing manner that few tourists realized that half of what he told them was made out of whole cloth.

One of his favourite tricks on this particular trip was to

have the cook fill a pitcher with condensed milk and place it on the table.

"Like to try a little of this, ma'am," Marion would say. "Real moose milk. It's in season right now. Try a little bit—you mightn't like it but it's an experience."

The tourists all tried the milk with various exclamations, some of delight, some of disgust.

"It tastes rather like condensed milk, doesn't it?" a woman from Philadelphia, who sat next to me, remarked.

"Yes, ma'am, that's what a lot of them say," Marion said in his slow drawl. "But strong—tangier-like."

"Yes it is—noticeably stronger," said the woman from Philadelphia.

"That's the woods flavour," said Marion. "Game flavour. Lot of people don't like it, but me, I prefer it to cow's milk. 'Course I been raised on it."

One of the most famous stories about Marion concerns a graveyard near the edge of the river, around Selkirk, I think, where the banks are very high. One day Marion got the boat to stop and took two sticks, which he hammered into the bank about three feet from the top. Then he tied a large miner's boot on to each stick. On the next trip, when the boat passed the bank, Marion strolled on deck and looked casually over the side among a group of tourists.

"Look there," he said. "By golly, that bank's eating right into the old graveyard. There's poor old Sam—they buried him with his boots on, y'know. Sliding right down the bank there. Shame, isn't it?"

The *Casca* was full of tourists on this trip, for August was the peak of the season. The boat stopped frequently for wood, for the upriver trips used a cord every hour. The wood was cut inland and hauled to the river's edge at periodic points all along the way. On our first morning out we stopped alongside a great pile of it. Out went the freight gangplank and then the deckhands, or "wood monkeys", began to trundle it into the bowels of the steamer by hand cart while the rest of us wandered up and down the bank in the sunlight. In the background, surrounded by a crowd of Malemutes, the woodcutter, a stooped and bearded man, was standing, checking to make sure the purser made an exact count of the amount taken. The company paid eight dollars a cord for wood and some of the piles contained more than two hundred cords, sawn into four-foot lengths. All day and all night long, as the steamboat moved upriver, we could hear the rumble below us as load after load of wood was run down to the furnace and thrown with a crash into the well, where the stokers waited for it.

There was always something doing on the river and the *Casca* was continually stopping or slowing down for some reason. Periodically the "wild-animal whistle", as the children called it, would sound and a herd of caribou would swim across our bow or flank, graceful creatures identical with reindeer, but very stupid and curious and as interested in us as we were in them. The steamer often had to make nearly a dead stop to avoid running them down. The whistle always sounded for animals—for a bear fishing alongside the river, a grizzly running up a bare hill with the speed of a deer, or a moose and its mate feeding placidly in the underbrush.

Occasionally, the *Casca* stopped to let off a man in the wilderness. There was one silent individual aboard known as "Stampede John", and one morning the steamer drew up alongside a bank where a little stream joined the Yukon and Stampede John got off with a year's grubstake in parcels and sacks. He was so nicknamed because he was supposed to have been on every stampede in the North, since the first one. Now, presumably, he was stampeding again. We left him there, all alone, surrounded by his bags and parcels, without a cabin or a trail in sight, a solitary man beside the river bank with the spruce and aspen stretching off for miles on all sides of him.

The Yukon is a lonely river and on this trip I came to realize how much it had become a river of graves and ghosts. The graves were dotted all along the banks, marked sometimes by a crude cross, sometimes by a bleached wooden slab, sometimes only by a mound. The Indian graves were more picturesque— little houselike structures built over the grave and surrounded by a fence to prevent animals plundering the gifts placed within for the souls of the departed. These gifts always included a plate, cup and spoon for the Indian spirits to eat with. Kid Marion had a story about an old Indian who, when asked why these utensils were necessary, replied that "spirits of my people come up to eat; spirits of white people come up to smell flowers."

Even more desolate than the graves were the empty cabins along the river, waist deep in weeds, their sod roofs caved in by the snows of winter, their doors and windows gone. Ghost cabins they were, and there were ghost ships, too, beached for ever, sitting up against the bank or bleaching like skeletons in the sun. Occasionally we saw a thin wisp of smoke curling up in the distance, serving to emphasize the emptiness of the land around us. Somewhere out there, lost in the waving ocean of spruce, there was a man living in a shack with only a Malemute dog for company. From the top deck of the boat the land seemed to roll off endlessly from the river bank, a rough carpet of dull green merging with the smoky mountains far in the distance. Except for the throbbing of the paddle wheel at the stern and the rumble of the wood below us, the world about us was as silent as the tomb. The boat would chug around each bend in the river and a new vista would unroll before us, as silent and as empty and as mysterious as the last.

Sometimes we came upon a river postbox, simply a gunny sack nailed to a tree, or half of a condensed-milk case perched up on the bank. The steamer would nose into shore and the purser would leap off and throw the mail into the box and then leap back on again. Only the box and a thin trail threading into the woods gave a hint that somewhere back behind the green cyclorama of wilderness there lay a pinpoint of civilization.

At Stewart City, where the Stewart River joins the Yukon,

the *Casca* picked up a long barge filled with sacks of silver ore that had been brought down the Stewart from the mines at Mayo and Keno Hill and was destined for trans-shipment to a smelter in Idaho. The sacks weighed one hundred and twenty-five pounds each and there were hundreds upon hundreds of them stacked neatly on the barge. Every one of them would have to be handled eleven times before it reached its destination and this explained why no ore worth less than a hundred dollars to the ton was considered worth mining. The barge was attached to the steamer's prow and we pushed it up the river ahead of us.

There were only two settlements along the river of any size, Selkirk and Carmacks, each consisting of a huddle of cabins strung out along the bank with a trading post at the centre. In the winter Indians camped around these settlements, but otherwise each consisted only of a couple of stores, a telegraph office, a mission and a dozen or so cabins half hidden in the greenery. There was a one-man detachment of the R.C.M.P. at each community, and as soon as the steamboat's whistle sounded, it was the constable's habit to run inside his post, doff his normal brown work coat and substitute the famous scarlet jacket that excited the tourists so much.

Of all the river settlements, only Selkirk dated far back before the gold rush. It had been a Hudson's Bay Company post in 1848 under Robert Campbell. After the post was attacked and burned by Indians, Campbell made a memorable trip by canoe and snowshoe to the nearest white settlement at St. Paul, Minnesota, more than three thousand miles away. Civilization was closer to Selkirk now, but looking at the cabins along the bank I reflected that they could not be greatly different from the log stockade that Campbell had built almost a century before.

Forty miles out of Selkirk the *Casca* forced its tortuous way through the narrow channel of the Five Finger Rapids. These rapids consist of four huge buttes jutting out of the river, leaving slender channels, or "fingers", between. The only navigable channel is on the north side of the river and it is barely wider than the steamboat itself. We soon learned the water was so swift that it was impossible for the *Casca* to go through unaided. A cable, anchored to the rocks above and below the rapids, was brought into play, passed through a winch in the *Casca's* bow, and the steamer hauled itself between the rock walls, its engines steaming and puffing as an officer on the barge in front recorded soundings every inch of the way. It took us two hours, in this manner, to go a few feet.

A few hours farther on, close to the town of Carmacks, we waved at a group of Indians drying fish near their cluster of tents in the woods beside the river. A man came down to the river with some ragged children and waved, too. With a shock, I recognized him. He was the son of a civil servant in Dawson and I knew his story well. He had been raised in the Yukon, running wild in the summer on the river, running wild in the winter through the snow. His family had sent him Outside to the university but he wouldn't stay. He came back to Dawson and went to work as a bank clerk, but he did not care to work behind the bars of a teller's cage. One summer his parents went Outside for a trip. When they returned they found he had married a half-breed girl. She was a pretty little thing, bright and neat, and I think could have made him a good wife, but the parents were so shocked they would neither see nor speak with him. This attitude drove him from the town and back into the bush, where his life was spent among the Indians, hunting and cutting wood for a living. Now here he was, standing by the river, with his dark, wiry children clustered about him, the fish wheel in the background turning slowly with the current, the salmon smoking under the trees. To all intents and purposes he was a native. I waved, remembering him as he had been, a neat boy in a white shirt in the teller's cage, with a wild look in his eye, and seeing him as he was now, tanned almost black, his hair long and stringy, his clothes worn and in tatters. He waved again, and then the boat was around the bend and the scene was wiped clean from the slate of the countryside.

And thus we chuffed upriver to Whitehorse. The following day we were aboard the train for Skagway, pausing at Bennett for the unvarying meal of moosemeat, beans, hash and blueberry pie. There was a monument over Dead Horse Gulch now and the train stopped so that we all might get out and read the inscription:

THE DEAD ARE SPEAKING. . . .
IN MEMORY OF US THREE THOUSAND PACK
ANIMALS THAT LAID OUR BONES ON THESE
AWFUL HILLS DURING THE GOLD RUSH OF
1897–1898, WE NOW THANK THOSE LIST-
ENING SOULS THAT HEARD OUR GROANS
ACROSS THIS STRETCH OF YEARS
WE WAITED BUT NOT IN VAIN
Placed by the Ladies of the Golden North
and the Alaska Yukon Pioneers.

We were in Skagway by evening and we made the most of our short time there, for Skagway had ceased to be the drab little town I had seen on my first trip north. Now it was a village dedicated entirely to preserving the memory of the town's leading moneymaker, the late Jefferson R. Smith, better known as "Soapy". In his lifetime, Soapy Smith, a confidence man from Denver, had gouged the Skagway visitors mercilessly. (He got his name from wrapping up soap with five-dollar bills, palming the money and selling each cake for a dollar apiece.) Now the citizens of Skagway were gouging the visitors in his name. Smith had operated a bar in which his luckless victims were fleeced. Now there was a bar containing life-sized dummies of Smith, where the tourists were fleeced at fifty cents admission each. There was also Soapy Smith's grave, well protected by wire mesh from souvenir hunters, and Soapy Smith's regularly freshened bloodstain on the wharf, to mark the spot where he had been shot to death by a vigilante named Frank Reid. (There was no wire mesh on Reid's grave because nobody wanted a souvenir of it.) There were postcards for sale showing Soapy Smith on a white horse and other postcards showing him dying on a white cot. There was a giant painting of his skull on the cliffs above the town, grinning down at the passers-by, so that it was impossible not to be aware of this desperado for a single moment of one's stay in Skagway. He was, indeed, Skagway's leading industry. Nay, he was her only one.

The following morning we left Soapy Smith behind and took the *Princess Louise*, a sister ship of the ill-fated *Sophia*, Outside. Was it significant that the Canadian Pacific had changed the schedule so that we passed down the Lynn Canal in the dead of night, thereby missing the scene of the tragedy, which was still marked at that time, if I recall rightly, by the death ship's masts, protruding from the water like grave markers?

For both children, who had never been out of Dawson, the Outside world was like a fairyland. They had never seen coloured lights or animated signs, for instance (not to mention street cars and railway trains). They could not understand why the people in the streets did not say hello to them, as everybody did in Dawson. They were excited when we promised to take them for a picnic on the beach, and disappointed when we got there. They had been used to picnics along the solitary rivers and creeks of the Yukon, and the seething mass of naked humanity on English Bay in Vancouver startled and terrified them. The idea of picnicking on a place where there was no grass, no trees and no fire, and where the water was black with people, was one they couldn't get used to.

In the rambling old Ontario orchard of their grandparents they were in their seventh heaven. It was the first time that either had realized that apples grow on trees. Only one thing bothered them: the fruit had spots and scales on it and at first they refused to eat it. For, of course, in Dawson we always got first-grade apples without a blemish. There were other novelties—earthworms, toads and snakes, all unknown in the North; their screaming terror at the sight of their first bulldog, for they had known only huskies; their delight at a playhouse covered with "real" grapes. They were, in fact, like children from another world and the Outside was a huge continual carnival to them. But as spring drew near, they began to grow restless, as I did, and cry openly for a return to the Yukon they knew.

Fourteen

WE RETURNED to Whitehorse again in early June, in time for the mosquitoes. Frank was waiting for us, bursting with the news that he had purchased a twenty-eight-foot boat for the voyage downriver. We would float back to Dawson, live in the open, go to bed in sleeping bags, eat meals on sandbars, catch fish and see wild animals.

"She's an old poling boat, the biggest I could find," Frank told us. "She's good and long and has a flat bottom. She hardly draws any water at all. That should make it easy at the rapids."

We were standing outside the White Pass Hotel, and looking up the street we now saw the familiar figure of Bishop Stringer striding towards us.

"What's this about the lot of you floating down the river in a boat?" the bishop asked.

"All the way," Frank said.

"I suppose you've got a good engine."

"No engine. We're going to drift."

"Well," said the bishop, "at least it has a poetical sound— 'drifting down to Dawson'. But what about Le Barge?"

"I'm fixed for that. I've got a sail I'm going to rig up. We came through that way in '98 in less time than you can shake a stick at."

"You must have had a good wind, that's all I can say. This time you may not be so lucky. You may find yourself rowing that boat for thirty miles."

"I doubt that."

"Well, if you do, watch out for squalls on the lake and keep well over on the left bank. And look out for snags in the main river. You know what they're like. Well, I'm off in a day or so myself, up the Pelly. Good luck to you."

The bishop turned towards the White Pass offices then stopped.

"Incidentally, have you got a good mosquito bar? No? Well, then, take my advice and pick one up at Taylor and Drury's. They're four-fifty and a bargain."

For this piece of advice we thanked the bishop and his Lord every night of the trip and for many nights thereafter.

The whole town had known of our expedition long before we arrived and most of the Whitehorse people thought we were utterly crazy. Many men and a few women had drifted down the Yukon river in a variety of craft, but this was the first time that a family of four, including two young children both under six years of age, had made the journey—and for fun.

"This is the craziest thing we ever did," I told Frank as we walked down to the river that evening to inspect the new boat.

"Nothing of the kind," Frank said. "Perfectly safe. Good experience for the kids." He paused on the bank and pointed down to the waterside, at a long, green craft bobbing in the river.

"There she is. Lots of room in that for the kids to play in. I got her from an old prospector for fifty dollars."

He jumped into the boat and did a sprint around the gunwale.

"See—she simply won't tip."

In the face of his enthusiasm I kept my peace, but secretly my mind was full of the darkest misgivings about this venture.

"You'll have to line up all the grub first thing in the morning," Frank was saying. "Make out a careful list and then double the order. That's what we did in '98."

Back at the hotel we found a mounted policeman waiting to see us. It was customary, he explained, for the force to keep details of all journeys down the river, the names of those participating, destination, estimated time of arrival, identification and so on. The suggestion made me uneasy. It reminded me of an operation I'd had when, just before going under the ether, a brisk matron arrived to ask me my religion and the names of my next of kin.

Our adventure began the next day at noon, the boat laden down with tent, sleeping bags, blankets, boxes of food, axe and shovel, pots and pans and toys for the children. Frank gave a hefty push, we swept away from the bank out into the main channel of the swift, glacier-blue river, and a moment or so later we were around the bend and alone with the wilderness.

It was a brilliant day with an exhilarating breeze, the atmosphere so clear that the snow-covered peaks sixty miles away and the closer granite mountains appeared almost unreal. I felt I was looking at a freshly painted stage curtain and the effect was enhanced by the new green of the spring foliage, the bright splashes of wild flowers on the banks and the coveys of swallows skimming by.

Swollen by spring freshets, the river sparkled and danced, gurgling under the boat's flat bottom and hissing from its hundreds of whirlpools. Logs, pieces of driftwood and whole trees torn up by the roots raced along with us. We passed a submerged island with only a few treetops visible; we grated on a sandbar; we got caught in an eddy under the bank. On we went, past sloughs, past islands, past thickly wooded gullies. An old man, sitting in the door of a mudroofed cabin, gazed at us without blinking. A group of brown little children ran down to stare at us from an Indian camp and scrambled for the oranges that we threw to them. A flock of duck rose from a quiet backwater between two islands and skimmed across our prow.

The children were tucked together into the prow of the boat. I sat amidships. In the stern, paddle in hand, watching the river, was Frank. I began to experience a sense of excitement and adventure, and the feeling of foreboding that had been strong within me at Whitehorse now passed.

As the warm afternoon sun rose in the sky, the children settled down on cushions in the bottom of the boat and went to sleep while I lay back on a roll of blankets and gave myself up to the shifting world of trees and rocks and islands and sky slipping past us. Soon I, too, dozed off.

Frank was calling out:

"It's nearly five. We ought to be looking for water. Keep your eyes peeled for a gulch and remember to tell me in plenty of time. I've got to get over to the bank, remember, and we can't navigate upstream."

"There!" I cried, pointing.

"No good. No shore for the kids to run. Anyway, you spoke too late."

Farther on we spotted a perfect cove. Here we filled our pails from a gurgling freshet.

"Let's camp here," I said. "It's lovely—and look at all those flowers."

"Camp here? Among all this green stuff? No thanks! We'd be eaten alive by mosquitoes. We'll have to find a sandbar in the middle of the river."

We finally found a wind-swept gravel bar devoid of both mosquitoes and kindling wood and here we camped. Frank took the boat for wood across the river, then cut poles for our ten-by-twelve tent, while I made supper. After the meal I cooked up a pot of porridge, clamped the lid on tight, covered it with an insulating garment of moss and buried it deep in the sand. In this primitive fireless cooker it would cook all night and be a fine thick jelly in the morning.

And here we slept through the bright northern night, rising early next morning to reach Lake Le Barge while the wind was fair. Yet, hurry as we did, it was still ten-thirty before we pushed off. In spite of the nomadic life, the same old round of housework—fires, meals, dishwashing—pursued us in the woods.

We fed well. We lunched that day on a long, clean sandbar and I cooked a substantial meal on a driftwood fire. I cooked soup, mutton chops with carrots and potatoes, boiled custard and preserved strawberries. It sounds simpler than it was. A swarm of houseflies descended on me as soon as I unpacked the meat. Half-way through the cooking operations the children buried each other in sand and had to be thoroughly whisked, washed, brushed and combed. Just as we sat down with a full dinner plate—on a table held down with stones and brushed clean of insects—a wind sprang up and we found ourselves caught in a river sandstorm. I have never since been able to eat a mutton chop without tasting grit.

That evening we camped at the entrance of Lake Le Barge, pitching our tent on a high bank above the river. As we ate supper, the thin drone of a motor-boat could be heard approaching. It was the first craft we'd seen since leaving Whitehorse, so we watched it with interest.

The boat contained four Indians. They tied up to the bank, climbed out, filed up the cliff, responded to Frank's greeting with the merest grunt, then plumped themselves down on the ground. I offered them supper; they shook their heads solemnly. We began to resume our meal; they sat and watched us silently. We occasionally tried to make conversation; they replied only with "yuh" or a "nuh". Yet they were obviously enjoying themselves, for their eyes followed our every movement with fascination. They sat thus for an hour watching us, then, as if by unspoken command, all four stood up at once and filed off as silently as they came.

Lake Le Barge is thirty miles long and up to five miles wide. It is ringed by mountains, and on the right-hand side they sweep right down to the water's edge to provide scenes of unparalleled beauty. As dangerous squalls spring up frequently, it was to the left side with its sheltered coves that we steered our boat the following morning. The wind was due south and Frank swiftly raised his sail. He had hardly done so when the wind switched to the north and to our disgust stayed this way for our entire trip down the lake. The sail, except for very brief periods, was useless and Frank had to bend to the oars. Instead of the five hours we had expected to navigate the lake in, we spent five nights on what Service describes as "the marge of Lake Le Barge".

At the head of the lake we had our lunch by an old derelict steamboat, half buried in the sand. This was the old *Olive May*, immortalized 15 years earlier as the *Alice May* in whose boiler Sam McGee was supposed to have been cremated. A man's body actually had been cremated in the boiler of the *Olive May*, by a Dr. Sugden, who was sent out from Whitehorse to give medical attention to a sick prospector. The man was dead and frozen stiff when Sugden arrived, and as he had no tools to bury the body, the doctor cremated it in the ship's boiler and brought the ashes back to town. Later, Sugden and Service lived together and this undoubtedly explains the origin of the ballad about the man from Tennessee who never could get warm enough in the Yukon.

When we were half-way down the lake I made the distressing discovery that our flour had disappeared. Undoubtedly we had left it behind at our last camp. We still had a good fifteen miles to cover before we reached Lower Le Barge, where we would buy flour and bread at the telegraph station.

"We'll have to speed up a little," Frank said. "In the meantime—rations. The children can have the bread that's left. We'll get by on biscuits and rice."

But it was another two days before we sighted the log cabin that houses the Lower Le Barge telegraph station. Fortunately we caught a salmon-trout two feet in length, which did us for three meals. Le Barge is noted for its fish, and as much as a ton and a half a week has been shipped from the lake to Dawson and Whitehorse.

We saw not a soul the entire length of the lake, which was as still and as empty of life as it had been in the days before the flotillas of the gold-seekers crossed it in June of '98. Only on the fifth day did civilization, in the form of the steamer *Casca*, cross our path. We looked up at the boat and waved to the tourists and they waved back, wondering, I have no doubt, who this strange family was, and what they were doing with two small children here in the wilderness. It occurred to me that they must have looked down upon us from the deck above much as I had looked down from the same deck upon the bank clerk who had gone native, as he and his children waved at the passing steamer.

At the foot of the lake we saw a single log cabin in a small clearing. This was the Lower Le Barge telegraph station and here we put in. We were mildly surprised to find that the telegrapher was expecting us. Indeed he knew all about us, as everyone on the river did. We had been so long coming down the lake that the police, who were always vigilant about such things, had become worried and wired ahead to the station to see if there was any word. In Dawson, I discovered later, we were given up for dead.

We pitched our tent on the bank in front of the telegrapher's cabin. Across the river, in the light summer dusk, a campfire glowed brightly. We waved at the two figures standing beside it, and they waved back. Then a boat moved out from the bank and came across to our side of the river. The two men in the boat turned out to be medical students from the University of California. They were travelling down the river peddling a medical book on home first aid, and from its proceeds they hoped to be able to make enough to continue their studies. At first, their trip sounded mad to us, as ours must have to them. But it turned out they were doing very well. The customers, to be sure, were few and far between, but every single man on the river had bought their book. This was not to be wondered at, for men were so glad to see anybody that the purchase of a book was a small-enough token of appreciation for the alleviation of their loneliness. Besides, it was a practical book for people living on the river without recourse to medical aid.

I was able to buy some flour at the station and the next morning we made our way to a pretty little island set in a maze of shallow sloughs. Here we decided to set up housekeeping for a couple of days. I had a good-sized bundle of washing to do as well as a batch of bread to make.

As we were using dried yeast cakes for the bread, the question arose as to how to keep it warm through the night. For although the days were hot enough to peel our faces with sunburn, the nights were chilly. We solved the problem simply enough by taking the bread to bed with us. There, wrapped in an eiderdown, along with a hot-water bottle, it reposed cosily until morning. Unsanitary, perhaps, but at least it rose.

After breakfast I made up the loaves in coffee cans and set them out in the sun. In the meantime Frank prepared an oven. First, he scooped a hole in the sandy bank and lined it with flat stones. Inside this he built a fire. When the stones and sand were thoroughly heated through he raked out the coals and inserted the covered tins of dough. He closed the opening with a large, flat stone and banked it with more hot sand. After an hour, I removed the loaves. I doubt if they would have won a prize in a baking contest, but they were good eating all the same.

The next section of the Yukon is known as the Thirty-mile and we found it the most scenic part of the entire trip. The swift, glacial water was a brilliant Mediterranean blue and so clear that gazing down into it we could count every pebble on the bottom. The beauty was deceptive, for the channel was narrow and the river a maze of snakelike twists. Captain Campbell of the *Casca* once told me he considered the Thirty-mile the most dangerous piece of river in the world. There are two tortuous hairpin turns on this river set so closely together that they form an almost perfect S. In the early days of navigation the pilots approached these bends warily at reduced speeds. Then one day a steamboat was sent out on an emergency call to aid a stricken sister vessel and the captain took the S at full tilt. This precedent has since been followed with safety. In our little boat there was less danger. Indeed, coasting down the swift, narrow Thirty-mile with its sudden twists and turns was quite like taking a long toboggan ride on a water slide.

At the end of the Thirty-mile at its junction with the Teslin we came to another famous old ghost town, Hootalinqua, at the end of the old Stikine Trail, one of the two "all-Canadian" routes of the gold-rush days. It was at this point that the men who came up through the wild interior of British Columbia (along the Stikine River to Telegraph Creek and thence overland to Teslin) reached the headwaters of the Yukon. In the spring and summer of '98 there had been thousands here; now there was only a handful of crumbling cabins and one old, unwashed man. He came down on to the bank and, as it was wet and chill, suggested we carry our blankets into the deserted telegraph station and camp there for the night. Then he disappeared.

We found several rooms containing bunks and took possession of one. Frank and the children were soon asleep, but I lay awake, listening to the familiar roar of the river, which had been part of my life for most of two decades. Suddenly, I heard the high-pitched whine of an approaching motor-boat. I peeked out, and to my astonishment saw a company of eight men jump ashore and come up to the cabin. Unaware of our presence on the ground floor, they trooped upstairs and began lugging down heavy boxes and packing-cases, which they hoisted into their boat. Then they built a campfire, cooked and ate an enormous supper and washed it down with several bottles of Scotch whisky.

I could contain my curiosity no longer and woke up Frank. He joined the party and found they were a big-game hunting expedition from New York headed by a man of great wealth, great vigour and great age, named Packard. He was eighty-seven. They had several guides and were heading up the Teslin. They had come here to Hootalinqua to collect their outfit, which had been freighted up ahead. They were off before we rose next morning.

As we continued to drift north, the days lengthened until there was no longer any twilight. Throughout the long midnight hours the broad daylight was enriched with the vivid colours of a continuous sunset-sunrise. These were beautiful evenings, and often we put the children to sleep in the bottom of the boat and drifted on down the silent river through the amber glory of sun and water. It was like a golden river now and we caught something of the feeling of enchantment.

One evening a little motor launch passed us on the other side of the river and two familiar figures in the back waved. They were Bishop Stringer and his wife heading on one of their restless trips up to the headwaters of the Pelly in the heart of the Rocky Mountains. The same evening we passed a camp on the bank and there were the two medical students sitting on the bank, reading their Bibles and waving to us. They were Seventh Day Adventists, and as it was Saturday, they were observing a day of rest.

The Yukon seldom runs in any direction for more than a quarter of a mile. Often the sun was behind us, then it would appear on our right or our left and occasionally, when the river turned south briefly, it would be directly in front of us. Low sandbars poked grey noses from the river in many spots and often the channel widened until it was a mile wide and choked with little islands between each of which ran a placid slough where ducks swam and sandpipers ran about.

On the twenty-first of June, the year's longest day, and a day we always observed by staying up all night, we drifted past a band of Indians camped on a bluff high above the water. They, too, were celebrating the solstice, dancing and singing around a bonfire to the music of a Victrola. The effect was stagelike: the black figures leaping and bounding against the firelight, the bright blue sky streaked with the orange of the brief sunset, the curiously incongruous sound of jazz filtering through the birch trees. Shortly after this we passed another ghost town, Little Salmon, once a prominent Indian village, now a graveyard, wiped out by the 'flu epidemic of 1917.

At three that morning we drifted silently in to the bank below the sleeping town of Carmacks, climbed up with our tent and pitched it in the middle of what passed for the main street. Nobody was surprised to find us there the following morning, for everybody knew we were coming and the town was expecting us. We stayed there half a day, picked up a haunch of moosemeat, then pushed on down the river.

We saw few people along the way, but when we did it was an event, for them and for us. At the mouth of the Nordenskiold River we saw a man standing on the bank, waving madly. He had obviously been watching for us.

"Come on over," he was calling. "Come on over and see us. Please come over."

We could not disappoint him. His name was Thayer and he owned a fox farm farther up the Nordenskiold. He insisted we go up to his house and have lunch. His wife, a lively New York woman, was starved for news—about styles, jazz, Whitehorse gossip, and the Outside. They lived in a luxurious house built of matched peeled logs, with a wide verandah enclosed in wire netting. There was a governess in residence in charge of several children. Why they were here in the wilderness raising foxes, I could not imagine, but looking over the house I could guess that the wife was probably more content than many city women in tiny apartments.

They had a young baby, and when I admired it she told me the child had been born in Whitehorse the previous winter. The question arose, of course, of bringing it home in the sub-zero weather. They had solved it simply. The new baby was tucked cosily into an egg crate and carried home in the Warm Storage Stage along with dozens of boxes of perishables bound for Dawson. This stage normally carried no passengers but was used to bring in eggs, fruit and certain vegetables, at proper temperature, and was kept warm with large charcoal heaters. The baby was dropped off sleeping cosily and peacefully at their doorway.

"Well," said Frank enthusiastically, as we pushed off again. "Five Fingers in the morning."

He saw my expression of foreboding and laughed.

"Nothing at all to it, as long as we're careful."

But my mind continued to dwell on the fate of those who hadn't been careful—or hadn't been lucky; Joe Wilson, for example, the postal clerk who sat at my table that first night in Miss Kenny's boarding-house. And there had been others.

We spent the night, an uneasy one for me, at Tantalus, another abandoned town, where the scar of a disused coal mine, one of the few in the Yukon, stood out blackly against the bright green of the hillside. Like almost everything else on the river, Tantalus was shut tight, the shafts crumbling, the buildings rotting away.

We were up next morning early; not at dawn, for dawn begins at one a.m., but before eight. Frank was working in the boat, preparing it exactly as he might have if he were about to take it over Niagara Falls. Everything, oars, boxes, luggage, tent, cushions, he tied down securely, generally clearing the decks of movable objects and packing all the small effects tightly into crates.

A short time later we were on the river again with the four black pinnacles of rock looming up directly ahead of us. In the morning sunlight the great rocks and the fingers of rushing water no doubt looked beautiful enough, but to me the high water caused by the June freshets, together with our rapidly accelerating speed, made the five channels seem unusually menacing.

"Look," said Frank, "I'll tell you what I'll do. I'll put you out on the bank and you can walk round the rapids and we'll pick you up on the other side."

I refused this suggestion. If we were to go to our deaths then, I said stoutly, we would go together.

The boat was racing now, fairly leaping through the rough water. The prow was pointing directly towards the centre rock and Frank kept it in this direction. I understood the manœuvre thoroughly, but still it dismayed me. We seemed about to crash into the granite pinnacle, though I knew that only by this method could we get into the current which would then sweep us through the narrowest of the five channels on our right. Many cheechakos in '98 took the widest channel as being the easiest and so met their deaths. The old river hands all knew that the narrowest channel was the deepest and best.

And now we were into it. At the last possible moment, the current seized us, twisted us over to the right and hurled us between the walls of rock now sweeping past us. We were met with spray and the roar of the water was loud in our ears. I squeezed the delighted children tightly to me and then, just as suddenly, we were through into the relatively calm water below. "Do it again, Daddy, do it again!" the children were squealing, but I was happy it was over safely.

A second set of rapids had to be navigated a few miles farther down—the Rink Rapids, less spectacular but considered more dangerous. In the early days the Government had spent a hundred thousand dollars deepening this section of the river, but it was still wrecking boats. We could see the hulk of the river steamer *Dawson*, wrecked the previous year, on the far bank. Some years later the *Casca* struck it and went down as well. But our own little boat passed through without incident.

Now the banks grew higher and a strange phenomenon appeared on them. Several feet down from the top, on either side of the river, was a wide, white streak, six feet deep, as if someone had drawn a giant whitewash brush along the bank for miles. This was a layer of volcanic ash, a reminder that once, hundreds of years before, a volcano had exploded and smothered half the Yukon in a hot, white blanket.

We were approaching Selkirk, at the mouth of the Pelly where it joins the Lewes River to form the Yukon proper, though actually the entire watercourse from Whitehorse down is known as the Yukon. Now the water, which had been bright blue, turned grey as the muddy Pelly joined with it. For the rest of its length the Yukon is muddy.

It was while we were camping at Selkirk that we heard reports about bears in the area. The storekeeper there told us a traveller coming upriver had seen seventeen of them, but

Frank claimed the children made so much clatter that we probably wouldn't be bothered.

That night we pitched our tent in a clearing near a forested hillside. Perhaps I had bear on my mind, but anyway I wakened at three o'clock to the sounds of a clattering of pots and pans outside, and the unmistakeable pad-pad of feet prowling around our tent. I was terrified, and reached to wake Frank, when the canvas began to shake violently and a large black snout appeared under it. I could feel my scalp prickle and my throat grow dry. I dug my fingers into Frank's shoulder and he let out an exclamation and jumped up. The snout vanished and by the time Frank was out of the tent there was no sign of a bear. Frank insisted I had dreamed it all until he saw the paw marks around the tent where the animal had tried to get at our box of bacon just under the canvas. The children slept on, oblivious to it all.

The next night the children remarked on the barking, or howling, of dogs in the distance. We could hear them over the hills quite distinctly, very like the huskies who howled at the moon in Dawson. It was not until the next day that Frank told me that what he had heard were timber wolves.

At noon the following day we reached Kirkman Bar, a treacherous obstacle on the river where as many as seven steamboats at a time have been trapped. Opposite the bar was the town of Kirkman, which consisted of a single cabin—a post office—and one curious man—the postmaster—who could now be seen standing on the bank and waving frantically to us. This was an old French-Canadian named Laderoute, a picturesque character in a loose blue blouse, with a long grey beard and huge gold rings dangling from his ears. A herd of goats and sheep followed him about like pet dogs, eyeing us curiously. We had interrupted his dinner and nothing would do but that we share it with him. We had already lunched but we knew better than to refuse river hospitality, and so we joined the meal, which consisted of porcupine stew, hot and very gamy, not unlike pork with a suggestion of chicken. As we sat down at the table we saw that the goats and the sheep had followed M. Laderoute into the cabin. Indeed, they never seemed to leave his side.

It was then that I recalled some of the stories I had heard about the postmaster of Kirkman. He claimed to be the seventh son of a seventh son, which, to a French-Canadian, meant he could put a curse on people. The steamboat men were afraid to cross him and sometimes the steamer wouldn't bother to put in for the mail because Laderoute would be standing on the bank calling down curses on one and all. There was plenty of free gold up Kirkman Creek and Laderoute, who did a little mining, would leave a poke of dust on the bank for the purser to collect when the boat stopped. The purser would weigh it out, sell it, and use the money to buy provisions, which he took back to Kirkman.

When Laderoute's son-in-law died in Montreal, he sent for his daughter to keep house for him. She was glad to come. Kirkman appears in large letters on the map and she assumed that her father was the wealthy mine-owning postmaster of a large and prosperous community. The steamboat dropped her off on the shore one dark night and she was faced with the strange old man, the single cabin and all the sheep and goats. In dismay and horror, she took the next steamer back for the Outside, but in Whitehorse met and married a fellow Quebecker and settled down there to a happy life.

"How about making Stewart our next camp?" Frank said, as we waved good-bye to Laderoute and his animals. "There are some fine mooselicks around there, and with a bit of luck——"

"With a bit of luck we might get home," I told him, for by now we had been more than two weeks on the river and I was anxious to return to a regular routine. "Stewart tonight, by all means; and then Dawson."

We decided, as a result, to drift all night until we reached Stewart City. Early that evening we passed the mouth of the Great White River, a watercourse which seemed to be flowing with pure milk, hence its name. Its startling colour comes from volcanic ash. The river is fed by glaciers and is thick with this white volcanic sediment.

It was nearly midnight when we approached the mouth of the Stewart River. We could hear it roaring far over on our right, but it was a wicked night and we could hardly see the far bank. The sky was black with storm clouds, the wind was coming in gusts and the rain was lashing down across our bow. It was now Frank's task to bring the boat around and try to get across the Yukon to the right bank, where the town of Stewart was located. This was rendered more than usually difficult by the wind, which was blowing us to the left, and the strong current of the Stewart coming from our right and pushing us in the wrong direction. In the uncertain light from the overcast clouds, distances were deceptive and objects hard to distinguish. I was glad the children were asleep.

"This is bad," Frank called from the stern. "Get up there in the bow and watch for floating logs. Sing out if you spot any."

By now the rain was driving down in sheets and it was impossible to see more than a few feet. The wind increased and we now met the full force of the Stewart current on the starboard. Despite Frank's frantic paddling we found ourselves washed into a shallow slough from which great snag piles stood out dimly against the sky. These snags are the most treacherous obstacles on the river. They are formed by the roots of trees and drifting logs piling up on the small sandbars season after season. The effect in the wet dusk was ghastly, for the skeletal branches and roots, bleached white by the elements and animated by the wind, seemed trying to clutch at the boat as Frank snaked in between them.

Suddenly, looming directly ahead, there appeared the silhouette of a terrible snag pile, twenty feet high—a thick, evil, shapeless tangle. The wind and current were blowing us directly on to it.

I screamed: "Frank! Quick!"

I could hear him mutter, "My God!" and gasp for breath as he renewed his efforts with the paddle. I held my breath as we plunged on, praying that he could keep us off.

Then, slowly, the gap widened and with just six feet to spare we swept past it and out into the main channel again. All this takes time to relate, but it happened in an instant and when it was over I was sweating heavily. It was, I recalled, almost at this very spot that Dr. Lachapelle had been drowned, under very similar conditions, I imagine.

Through the rain we could now see the lights of the road-house at Stewart. This in itself shows how dark this particular June night was. We decided at once to spend the rest of the night under a roof, for we were all in and had no stomach for a tent. It was, as it turned out, the most uncomfortable night we spent on the river. The four of us were crammed into one tiny room infested with mosquitoes, and we had left the mosquito bar in the boat. I didn't get much sleep.

Stewart City consisted of about a dozen cabins, a general store, a post office and a telegraph station. It had once been a thriving mining community in the days before the gold rush, but the Klondike strike turned it into a ghost town. It was set on an island, in the angle between the two rivers, with a shallow slough running behind it, and it faced certain extinction because the angry Yukon was eroding the banks of this island at the rate of several feet a year, causing all the buildings to be moved back periodically towards the slough. It was a moot question whether the river or the general decay would destroy it first.

The last seventy-mile stretch of river was quiet and un-eventful. We left Stewart about noon. At three the following morning we saw once again the grey roofs and clustered cabins of Dawson City nestling under the scarred Midnight Dome. After the river settlements it looked like New York, with its big grey warehouses and its Government buildings and its ferry tower and its checkerboard streets.

Our arrival was timed for early morning at my insistence,

for I had no wish to meet the inevitable throng of townspeople on the river bank, dressed as we were in our soiled khaki outfits, I in baggy bloomers and the children looking like unkempt Indians without being half as picturesque.

The town was sleeping when we slipped in to the bank and tied up the boat. The sun was brilliant, the robins singing and the streets fragrant with the scent of briar roses. We made our way through the willows edging First Avenue and, with our gear on our backs, walked up the hill to home. A feeling, half of relief, half of elation, not unmixed with a certain sadness, came over me as we entered the house. I was beginning to realize that these two weeks had been among the happiest of my life. All this took place almost thirty years ago, but the memory of those lazy days drifting with the current through that silent, wild country, with my children young and my husband in his prime, has never left me, and remains as vivid and as sharp as if it all happened a week ago. Wishing is futile, I know, but I would give a great deal to be able to do it all again.

Fifteen

Once again our lives were ordered by the seasonal cycle of first and last boat, break-up and freeze-up, around which existence in Dawson revolved. Nature was our master, and we were prisoners of her rigid system. There were really only two seasons that counted in the Klondike, summer and winter. Autumn and spring passed so swiftly that it was hard to say when they began or ended.

Our seven months of winter confinement began the moment the final series of blasts from the whistle of the last boat floated across the town. From our windows we could see the steamer's lights moving slowly up the river and round the bend. Now that we knew who was leaving and who was staying behind we lost no time getting out our Christmas invitations, for there would be little further change that season in the make-up of the town's population.

The dark days were upon us. By mid-November the sun, which for weeks had been dropping lower over the southern horizon in an ever-narrowing arc, disappeared for two months and was not seen again until mid-January. This meant that, although we were by no means in perpetual darkness, we were in a sort of perpetual twilight. The children left for school in the bright moonlight and returned in the pitch dark. The street lights went on at three-thirty in the afternoon and in the houses the lights were kept burning nearly all day.

On cold nights the northern lights swept in their full majesty over the entire arc of the sky. They shifted in long, coloured bars, swirled on the horizon like flames or hung from the heavens in fringed curtains of electric green. They were mysterious and ghostly, always changing, never still. There was a great controversy over whether or not they could be heard crackling. Frank and I always planned an experiment in which I would be blindfolded and we would walk up the hill and watch the lights and, if I heard them crackle, I would kick him. But we never got around to it.

In the very cold weather a thick fog settled over the Yukon valley. It appeared as soon as the thermometer sank below forty, and, looking out from our windows, we could pretty well judge the temperature by its density. If the houses a short block away were invisible we knew it was forty below. If those half a block away were invisible it was fifty below. If Service's cabin across the street was shrouded, then we could be certain it was fully sixty below zero.

The thermometer could rise or drop with great swiftness. In the spring I have seen it go from forty below to thirty-five above in a few hours. In the dead of winter I have seen it go from twenty above to fifty below within two days. The lowest recorded temperature on the Government thermometer in Dawson was sixty-nine below zero, but the German consul in the early days had a very good thermometer, especially tested at the Leipzig Laboratories, which once registered seventy-two below. One December, the mercury hovered at fifty below for the entire month. There was a 'flu epidemic that year and there were many deaths, especially among the half-breeds and Indians, but there could be no burials until the weather moderated. The frozen bodies were stacked in the undertaking parlour. Indeed, the winter's graves always had to be prepared in the fall, when the ground could be easily worked. As more people died during the winter than during the summer, there were always a good many standing open ready for the season. It was a grisly sight to pass the rows of yawning holes waiting for occupants, and to wonder which of us would rest in them before the long winter was over.

Yet I cannot remember our children staying away from school because of the cold. They seemed impervious to it and on the coldest sub-zero days would play cheerfully in the snow-drifts that filled the ditches. We wrapped them up warmly. They wore two pairs of heavy woollen stockings under their felt boots and two huge pairs of mitts on their hands. Their heads were swathed in wool mufflers under their double woollen toques and their coonskin coats were tied with a second muffler around the waist. Thus attired, they waddled awkwardly to school, leaving vapour trails behind them, and looking like small woolly bears.

When the temperature dropped below sixty, the R.C.M.P. put a ban on all horses working out of doors, for they contracted pneumonia easily in the very cold weather. (Humans had to move carefully and slowly, too, for over-exertion or heavy breathing could freeze the lungs.) This meant we got no water. The only thing to do was to melt snow by the bushel, and for Frank to lug frozen pails of drinking water up from the Government building that was served by the one water main that ran all season.

Frank, as I have already indicated, had an inventive mind. He was always devising gadgets of one kind or another, and one winter, during a long spell of fifty-below weather, he made himself a stick-pin out of frozen mercury. First, he sharpened the end of a piece of brass wire, and roughened the opposite end. Then, using an R.C.M.P. button, he placed the rough end of the wire into a plaster mould, and filled the mould with liquid mercury. This he placed on the verandah, where at forty below it soon froze. He was soon sporting a unique piece of jewellery, a rare grey stone embellished with a buffalo head. He wore this proudly on his overcoat for a couple of weeks, then one evening forgot to take the usual precaution of jabbing the pin on the outside of the door before entering the house. Soon all that was left was the brass pin and a few droplets of quicksilver on his coonskin coat.

Forty below sounds cold, and it is, but the odd thing was that after a few weeks of fifty- and sixty-below weather, when the spirits in the thermometer rose to forty human spirits rose as well and the weather felt quite mild. We grew restive in out wrappings, loosened a scarf, unfastened a button or two, and remarked that it felt like spring.

We could never quite keep the cold or frost out of the house. It seemed an animate thing, creeping insidiously under the crack of the door in a long white streak. Each nailhead in the strapping around the kitchen door was covered by a little coat of ice, and the keyholes and knobs were always frosted over in the cold weather. A thick line of frost marked the lower edge of the door, and we could judge the temperature by gauging the distance this white line crept up along the door's edge from the floor to ceiling. The windows, of course, were always covered in a thick sheath of ice.

Our house was hermetically sealed, as far as possible, in the winter months. Each fall we pasted every window down with heavy paper so that no breath of air could enter. Our only ventilation was in the bedroom, where Frank had an ingenious arrangement above the bed consisting of a length of stove pipe stuck through the wall with a tight lid on a hinge which could be opened or closed by pulling on a rope to admit an icy blast of air.

We needed no refrigeration, of course. Anything placed on the back porch froze solidly at once. Usually it was too cold to make proper ice cream, but whenever the weather grew milder I simply mixed up some cream and flavouring, placed it on the porch for a few minutes and then brought in a ready-made frozen desert. We kept a box of blueberries on the porch all winter from which we helped ourselves from time to time. In addition, we usually had the carcass of a caribou which Frank had shot the previous fall. He would bury the caribou where it dropped, for the ground being frozen solidly under the surface made any hole a perfect refrigerator. After freeze-up he would return and dig it up and bring it back frozen solid. We would spend a terrible night in the kitchen hacking it up with saw, hatchet and knives and packing it between layers of snow in a box to be placed on the porch.

Hardly a winter passed without some tragedy brought on by the cold. Every season several men went missing in the hills above Dawson or along the Klondike. The following spring, their corpses or their skeletons would be found among the foliage. One spring a man was found dead in Thomas Gulch on the hill above us, not more than half a mile from our front door. He had simply lain down in the snow and died of exposure.

There was a curious tragedy at Gold Run, near Granville, one winter. A Mexican named Sam Tim had stumbled out of the house of Gypsey, the local demimondaine, after a hard drinking bout, and simply vanished into thin air. Parties searched the district and the police combed the countryside, but there was no trace of him. It was an eerie business and people avoided going past his cabin as a result. The mystery was solved the following spring when the snow began to melt. Sam Tim's horrified brother found him not far from his cabin encased in a solid block of ice, staring out from this prison with wide-open eyes, as if he were still alive. He had apparently lain down in the snow, being under the influence of liquor, and frozen to death. A spring of fresh water under the trail had frozen into a glacier all around him and the snow had covered the glacier up. Now here he was, staring out of the ice at the crowd that gathered, looking just as he had in life except for the slight distortion of his crystal prison.

Another winter, poor old Smith Constance fell a victim to the cold. He was the ex-newspaperman whom Frank and I had sometimes stopped to talk with on Sourdough Gulch. He had long been destitute, his normally ragged clothed looking more ragged than ever, and in his final years the Yukon Government helped him out with supplies of groceries and tobacco. It was while fetching home these provisions to his claim on Bonanza one Christmas that he met his death. It had been a pleasant-enough Christmas Eve, not more than thirty below, but towards night when Constance started to head home the thermometer began to drop. He was eighty years old and he probably became numb and dazed with cold and fatigue as he neared his cabin. At any rate they found him lying not fifty yards from his door, his tracks in the snow tracing an aimless path around a little fir tree.

The Yukon was as ruthless as that, and we became accustomed to such tragedies each winter. Some froze inside their own cabins because they would lie down on their bunks exhausted, the fire would go out and the cold would creep in and kill them. Occasionally, too, the R.C.M.P. would come across a strange, parka-clad figure standing stiffly in the snow, unmoving. This would be the corpse of a man who had stopped to knock his numbed feet together and wipe the ice from his stiffening eyeballs, only to find that he could not move on. And there he would remain, a grisly statue in the gathering dusk.

Christmas and New Year's marked the peak of the winter season. In late December the town had a Christmas-card feeling to it, the snow crisp and glistening in the moonlight, the air clear, and each evergreen tree outlined in powdery white. All over the valley you could hear the tinkle of sleigh bells and the air was pungent with the smell of freshly cut evergreens. Christmas had none of the slick, commercialized atmosphere that it has on the Outside. We had no radios to deafen us with incessant carols, and when we heard them in church the Sunday before the Yule, they fell sweetly upon the ear. We cut our own Christmas tree from the hills above, plunging through the deep snow to select a perfect specimen and dragging it back in triumph to the house. The town combined a few days before the holidays to hold a giant community Christmas party at which every child was given a present from an enormous tree that stretched thirty feet into the rafters. The day after Christmas, the hills were noisy with the cries of the half-breed children from the hostel, who were always given skis as presents by the hostel. For two weeks they slid down the hill, and then the skis mysteriously disappeared, to reappear on the feet of other children the following year.

New Year's Eve was marked by the most elaborate ball of the season, a fancy-dress affair in the A.B. Hall. The costumes were ingenious, and many people spent months working on them, for they were, of course, all hand-made. I remember men going as glasses of beer, complete with foam, as huge thermometers and as slices of water-melon. One year I went dressed as a T. Eaton Co. mail-order parcel (designed by Frank) addressed to Dawson City. The following day every man in town went on a round of visits from house to house while the women stayed home to receive and be kissed by all of them.

In the middle of January, the first rays of the sun would peep tentatively over the hills and for moments a tiny sliver of light would fall on Fifth Avenue in the centre of town. With this gesture in the direction of far-off spring, our spirits would commence to rise, and the sun and its progress across town would be the only subject of conversation for days.

"Sun's back. Isn't it great?"

"Say, isn't it fine to see the sun again?"

"I had a bit of it in my window today. Has it reached your place yet?"

"Be careful, you'll get a sunstroke."

Now for the first time in almost two months, people could again see their shadows. More and more of us would venture out into the streets to look at the phenomenon and at the tints of rose, gold and salmon once again painting the white hilltops.

Winter gave way to summer with only a cursory nod at spring. Suddenly one day the snow would go soft—all winter it had been as dry as sand—and down from the hills would pour scores of miniature cascades. The ditches in town would come into their own, filling to the brim with water. The low spots would become ponds, black with mosquito larvae and polliwogs and edged with snipe. The wild crocus would be peeking above the snow before it vanished, and then, as the final patches diminished on the hills, the ice would move in the Yukon and the water in the mains would be turned on again. This and the first boat marked the opening of summer.

The ice went out sometime during the first two weeks of May, and the moment of its break-up was one of the great events in Dawson. For weeks before, thousands of bets were laid on the exact day, hour and minute of its going, and I suppose there would be ten thousand dollars at stake in that town of eight hundred souls. The big Ice Derby, or "pool" as it was usually called, paid upwards of three thousand dollars to the man who guessed closest to the exact moment of the break-up. In addition, there were dozens of smaller pools all over town. Every store had a pool, based on the minute or the half-hour or the hour that the ice would move. The men at the Government buildings had a pool, the police had a pool, the hospital patients had a pool and even the school children had a pool. Frank organized a pool at home—four chances based on the quarter hour. In fact there was hardly a man, woman or child in town who hadn't gambled something on the time the ice would break.

The news that the ice was moving flashed through the town like an electric current. The time was fixed exactly in this manner. A Union Jack on a stake was frozen into the river in front of the town early in the spring, about a hundred and fifty feet from the shore. This was connected by a wire to a point on the Canadian Bank of Commerce building, on shore, in such a way that when the ice moved a hundred feet, a switch closed an electric circuit, stopping a clock in Charles Jeanererette's jewellery store and setting a gong ringing. Almost instantly the whistle in the fire hall on Front Street would sound and then the school bells, followed by the church bells. By this time, every husky dog from Lousetown to Moosehide was howling madly and the entire town was pouring down to the river.

On certain years the ice would go during the night, and when this happened the townspeople would leap from their beds and rush hastily clad to the water's edge. Once or twice the ice went on a Sunday morning, and then the entire church congregation flowed from the pews before the sermon had ended. The famous instance occurred almost immediately after the minister had given a violent sermon on the evils of gambling, with special reference to the ice pools. The choir had hardly started the hymn "Shall We Gather at the River" when, appropriately, the dogs and sirens indicated that the ice was moving. The entire church was empty in a moment and the clergyman himself reluctantly followed his parishioners to the waterfront.

The sight of the ice moving was a spectacular one. The great cakes, three to eight feet thick, roared down the river, smashing and grinding against each other with the noise of a dozen express trains. Often entire cakes would be hurled into the air until the banks on both sides of the river were piled with them, sometimes to the height of fifty feet. Occasionally, caribou could be seen clinging to the ice blocks as they swept by, or floundering in the water between them. Uprooted trees and the odd empty boat jammed into the ice would go sailing past the town. There were certain years when the ice jammed above the town, acting as a natural dam and raising the head of water until, with a terrible roar, it was unleashed to fall upon the swampy flats of Dawson, smashing wharves and splintering buildings and immersing the lower half of the town in four to six feet of water.

The opening of the river brought a new feeling to the town. It was a symbolic act of nature, akin to the breaking of bars on a prisoner's cell. A short time later the first boat puffed in, bringing with it the first fresh fruit we had seen for months. I cannot remember a more cheerful sight than that first steamboat with its high plume of white smoke and its yellow stack and bright red paddle-wheel, all newly painted, coming round the bend or standing at the dock. No one could tell for certain exactly when it would arrive, but the sound of its whistle again brought the whole town racing to the river. Apple Jimmy's stalls were soon stocked with peaches, grapes and bananas, for which we had been starved since the previous fall. In spite of the outrageous prices he was quickly sold out. On first-boat days school children were given a holiday and men left their desks and work benches. The sound of that panting steamboat put summer into the hearts of all of us.

With the opening of the river navigation Dawson's tourist trade began again. This was the one business that continued to flourish when others declined. The tourists to us were creatures from another world, although we knew most of their names and quite a bit about them. They stayed in town for forty-eight hours and often arrived in heavy fur coats when the summer temperatures were nudging the nineties. You could always tell a tourist, not only by his dress and appearance but simply because he didn't greet you in the street as the townspeople did. We saw a great deal of them, of course, because our house was opposite Service's cabin and they all visited that.

The cabin had been enshrined by the I.O.D.E. and it certainly paid for its keep. Those in charge on tourist days claim that the place was exactly as the poet left it, but this was something of an exaggeration. We had seen to it that the tourists got their money's worth and the two rooms, as time went on, became filled with such furnishings as a true Yukon poet should have, even if he didn't. There was the characteristic bunk, home-made stool and chair, gold-pan, miner's candlesticks and several glass-bowled coal-oil lamps. On the walls still hung some of the scraps of wallpaper on which Service had written his first drafts. By this time they were only scraps, for most of it had been carried away by souvenir hunters. Before Service left the Yukon to cover the Balkan wars he wrote the poem "Good-bye Little Cabin, Good-bye", and these verses had been framed and hung on the log wall of the porch.

On boat days the town was always full of strange people, their noses pressed against the jeweller's windows, seeking to buy nugget spoons, nugget ear-rings, nugget cuff-links, nugget stick-pins and nugget watch-chains. Every Saturday night the town held a "tourist dance" to which most of us turned out, for there were usually two boatloads in during the weekends. The other big attraction for the tourists was Mrs. George

Black, who had received considerable publicity Outside. She quite enjoyed it. On tourist days she would sometimes be discovered grubbing about the town's ditches looking for four-leaf clovers to put on place cards for her next party. It always delighted her when tourists approached and asked where they could find Mrs. Black. She would give careful directions, then speed home, put on a crisp and expensive gown and make an appearance before the discomfited strangers reclining in her garden.

Because of the perpetual light, those plants that would grow at all in the Klondike grew to enormous proportions. We had pansies four inches across, sweet-pea hedges ten feet high with as many as six flowers to a stem, and asters as big as chrysanthemums. The east side of our house was covered in the summer with canary vine which ran over the roof. Frank, with a scientist's curiosity, measured its growth one June twenty-first. It had grown five inches in twenty-four hours. All the annuals grew and flowered swiftly, but the perennials, except for delphiniums, which survived the hardest winters, were another matter. We did raise fine Canterbury bells and hollyhocks, but only by keeping them in the cellar from fall to spring.

Most of our seeds were planted in flats in March from earth stored over the winter in the cellar. They were transferred into dozens of old tins and set against the windows until the ice was out of the river in May. Then into the garden they went. The vegetables grew as rapidly as the flowers and matured so quickly that they were wonderfully tender and sweet. One of our neighbours grew a cabbage that weighed fifty pounds and we raised a cauliflower which weighed eleven pounds ready for the pot. Green peas grew well, but beans we couldn't grow at all. Our finest crop was spinach, which we gathered by the bushel and bottled for winter use.

On the hot summer's days we roamed the Yukon hills in search of berries, and these gypsy wanderings area mong my happiest recollections of the North. From the tops of the hills we could look out on a vast sea of wind-swept mountain tops billowing around us to the far horizons: in the east the glittering, snow-capped peaks of the Canadian Rockies; in the west the blue-purple ranges of Alaska. By midsummer, these hills were thick with berries: currants hanging in shiny clusters of scarlet and black; raspberries ripe for the eating; and masses of cranberries. Later on the blueberries hung thickly on the bush, so thickly that we used a box with a sharp tooth to comb out the shrubbery for faster picking. When the season was on the whole town took to the hills, each family slipping by devious trails and pathways to its secret patch, parents warning their children in stage whispers never, never to shout when picking or reveal by word or action the location of their private horde.

On these excursions we wore our oldest clothes and looked exactly like hoboes. I will never forget the Sunday afternoon when Frank and I and the children were prowling through the wreckage of Klondike City heading for the berry patches on the plateaus beyond and came face to face with the most fashionable couple I have ever seen, she in an expensive afternoon dress, wide hat and parasol, he in morning clothes and gloves. This was Lady Byng of Vimy, the wife of the governor-general of Canada, and an aide. Each governor-general invariably visited Dawson sometime during his five-year term of office, and the previous week the entire town, dressed in its best, had turned out to welcome the Byngs. Frank, I remember, had been president of the local Legion branch that year and we had both been presented to the vice-regal party at an elaborate reception that evening. Baron Byng had gone off on a hunting expedition and I thought the whole retinue had gone, too, but now here we were, looking worse than tramps, face to face with the First Lady of Canada. We carried on a brief stilted conversation (while the aide looked down his nose at us) and then fled to the hills.

After our trip down the Yukon we were hopelessly wedded to the river, and Frank, who could build anything, determined to build a boat. Accordingly, one spring he got the use of the old Klondike Hotel on Front Street and went to work on a twenty-six-foot, round-bottomed motor launch. The result was a thing of beauty and entirely his own doing, for he even soaked and bent the ribs himself. He named her *Bluenose*, after his native Maritimes, clamped a Johnson Seahorse Twelve on her stern and launched her, one bright June day, at the foot of Church Street. From then on we lived on the river during the summer months.

At the beginning of each season it was our habit to scout the river above the town for a suitable island. (We almost always journeyed upriver so that in case of a power failure we could always float back home again.) This island we claimed for our own, and established a camp on it. As the islands shifted every season it was impossible to establish a permanent river camp, but as there were plenty of islands we had no trouble finding what we wanted each June. Usually we chose one which had been partially under water in the spring floods, for when the river dropped it would leave large, warm pools behind that served as protected swimming areas all summer long. One could never swim in the river proper, of course. It meant almost certain death from undercurrent and exposure.

Here on our island we were kings of all we surveyed. Most of the islands were several miles in size and once we had established a camp nobody disturbed us. We could come and go as we pleased, doing and wearing what we wanted without interference. Here we spent all our week-ends and holidays, using the island as a base of exploration to roam up and down the river, through its innumerable sloughs and channels, and up its dozens of small tributaries. These lazy summer days, sitting back in the boat as it cruised slowly against the current, or lying full length on the hot sand of an island beach, are among my happiest memories of the North.

The river was alive with animals in the summer, wolves and coyotes howling at night, lone moose standing dramatically against the sunset, caribou swimming against the current by the thousands, and bears on the distant hills. Most of the bears were the ordinary brown or black variety that one was apt to find among the blueberry patches. They were as wary of humans as we were of them and both parties usually fled one another immediately after the initial encounter. The grizzlies though, were a different matter, and I was always nervous of them, with good reason. We saw them occasionally, always in the distance, huge animals rising on their haunches, the brown markings on their great flat faces easily visible at half a mile.

There was an old sourdough named Red MacDonald, a white-headed Scotsman of seventy-five, who lived in a little cabin perched on the bank some forty miles above Dawson and whom we used to visit during our longer boat trips. "Old Red", as they called him, was a silent, reserved man and nobody knew much about him. On his rare visits to town he usually brought us a brace of ducks or a ptarmigan and inquired after the children in the shy, hesitant manner of men who live alone. He had a patch of well-tended garden, I remember, where he grew his own potatoes, cabbage and celery. He was pretty well self-sufficient, even making his own jelly in glasses that consisted of beer bottles with the necks broken off.

We talked occasionally of the joys and penalties of living alone and I once asked him if he wasn't afraid of bears. He gave me a long look of simple incredulity and I felt a fool for posing the question. Yet, in the end, it was a bear that did away with him. One September morning, a month after our last visit, he walked down to the creek below his cabin to fill a pail with water. He never finished his task. An enormous grizzly tore him to pieces as he stooped over the pool, and left him sprawled and partially devoured on a carpet of yellow aspen leaves on the banks of the gulch. A woodcutter found him later that day and rushed back to camp for help. The men gathered up the remains in a piece of canvas, removed them to the cabin, and in case the grizzly returned barricaded the door. But when the police arrived, the barricade had been pulled aside, the door torn off, and the rest of the remains devoured. Only the mangled head lay on the floor. This leaves no doubt at all that, when driven to it, grizzly bears will attack human beings for food.

Nature does everything on a huge scale in the North, and the caribou migrations across the river were proof of it. Towards fall they would run in gigantic herds on their seasonal trek south from the tundra land. The paths of previous treks were easily discernible along the river bank, for the caribou trampled everything before them and ran in groups of hundreds and often thousands. I remember Guy Lewington telling me in the old days how he once narrowly escaped being trampled by a herd that he estimated contained fully five thousand animals in a solid mass.

The caribou's path shifted through the years, but during the late twenties their trails moved close to Dawson and we could see them plunging through the underbrush, or scrambling up the steep bank, from our vantage point on the river. Occasionally we would come upon a lost or abandoned calf left alone on a sandbar crying its heart out, and as fall progressed the entire river was pungent with the odour of decaying corpses where dying caribou, injured by wolves or accidents or careless hunters, had dropped along the banks and were rotting among the willows. After each year's treck there would be a new swath cut into the hillsides, the trees trampled and broken as if by a bulldozer and the beaches churned up by thousands of hoofs.

One hot afternoon we drove the boat into the midst of several dozen caribou swimming the river. We were so close that the children reached out and touched the velvet of their horns. This was a dangerous thing to do, for a herd could panic easily and swamp the boat. There were some visitors with cine-cameras a few miles down the river and Frank used the boat to herd the caribou down for their benefit.

As I've said, almost all our excursions were made upriver, for we didn't relish the idea of a power failure that would send us drifting down to Alaska (it was a straight two thousand miles of swift water to the Bering Sea). But one day Frank assured us that everything was running fine, so we decided on an excursion to Fort Reliance, eight miles below Dawson, an old trading post from the pre-gold-rush days now reduced to one cabin. As an added treat we took along Grey Cloud, our husky, who was seldom allowed in the boat but was always pleading to come.

It was only when we were returning that evening that I noticed a worried expression on Frank's face that clearly spelled engine trouble. Sure enough, the engine—and our hearts—missed a beat or two. One lung had given out. "We'll be lucky if we make Moosehide," Frank said.

We took advantage of the quiet shore eddies and had barely reached the outskirts of the village when, with a weak wheeze, the motor gave out. Frank seized the paddle and, before we could be swept out into the current again, made for the bank. An hour's work with the engine showed it needed a thorough overhaul by a skilled mechanic. We would have to walk to Dawson. Frank picked up our youngest and we headed through the little Indian village.

Just then a dog began to howl, a low, ugly sound. Grey Cloud's fur rose. Then another took up the cry . . . and another. Now I remembered the stories of the Moosehide Malemutes, stories of town dogs that had been attacked and torn to pieces by the "Indian dogs", which were of the same breed but, because of harsh treatment at the natives' hands, of a vicious temperament.

"Don't say a word," Frank said under his breath. "Keep a tight hold of Cloud and take this stick."

The village consisted of one short row of log cabins set on the bank at one end of which was the Anglican church and mission house. Below, cluttered up with fishing nets, fish racks, piles of old cans and dumps of filthy refuse, was the beach. Each armed with a heavy club, and with Grey Cloud held firmly in the centre, we advanced to face the music.

These Indian dogs had a fierce reputation throughout the Territory and they were known to spring instantly on dog or unprotected human. We could see their dark forms now steadily advancing from each cabin, into the main roadway. Huskies and Malemutes cannot bark or growl. Like wolves they can only howl, and it was this eerie, banshee sound, very low, which sprang now from their throats.

The sticks, and in the end the Indian bucks, protected us. At the outset of the hubbub not a soul was to be seen, but as the noise mounted, and as we began to club each dog as it advanced towards us, first one then another human figure slouched from each tightly shut cabin, seized the heavy stick that always reposed at the doorway for just such emergencies and began to flail at the snarling canines. Slowly the animals receded before this new wave of humanity, their black lips curling back over their teeth, and thus the village was breached in safety.

We ate a midnight lunch of left-overs on the crest of the shoulder of the hill overlooking Dawson and then, soothed by the panorama of golden sky and golden water, we proceeded down the rocky slide to home. But the Malemutes of Moosehide had their innings. When Frank went down next day to retrieve the crippled *Bluenose*, he found that they had clawed open our entire stock of emergency tinned rations and devoured the contents. I had an uneasy feeling that they had even managed to eat some of the tins themselves.

By mid-August we knew our river trips were drawing to a close for another year. For August is autumn in the Klondike. The town's great fall celebration came on August 17, the anniversary of the discovery of gold. Then the old pioneers held their parade and the children ran races and the garden harvests were exhibited and judged. Sometimes there would be few vegetables and flowers to display, for killing frosts could strike before mid-August, just as snow could fall in early September.

We beached our boat as the leaves grew sere on the trees, and began to hammer down the storm doors and windows and paste the heavy strips of brown paper over the cracks. Then we prepared for the ultimate ritual of the dying season: the pilgrimage to the dock to watch the last boat leave town, with its cargo of people who would never come back to Dawson City. I always thought it significant, though perhaps accidental, that while the first boat always seemed to arrive at eleven o'clock in the morning, the last boat invariably left at night. It slipped out into the dark river like a floating spectre, and as we waved it good-bye we adjusted ourselves mentally to our own long seasonal night, before the bright morning of another summer.

Sixteen

DAWSON CITY was like Sam Tim, the man frozen into the block of ice. It lay in a sort of state of suspended animation, its character, its people and its folkways frozen into an inflexible pattern by the constrictions of geography, climate and history. The town itself seemed much the same as it had in the gold-rush days, until you looked at it closely and found that the buildings were warped and aged and the frost had heaved the foundations so they were all on a slant. This gave a queerly distorted effect to Dawson, as if one were viewing it through a slightly warped mirror, or through a crystal cake of ice. So, too, were our customs and traditions fixed and immutable, if slightly distorted. On New Year's Day, for example, the men donned formal dress, pocketed their cases of engraved cards and went calling from house to house, where the women received them. They had been doing this, with little variation, since the turn of the century. No ball was complete without its grand march and its minuet, and the prescribed refreshments at bridge parties were exactly what they had been when I first arrived: sherbet, salted almonds, Turkish Delight.

In a sense, Dawson was a transient town, for although the population was now only a few hundred people, we still had seven flourishing hotels. But the transients made no dent in our social armour. The tourists, the police, the nurses, the teachers, the mining men and ministers all ebbed and flowed through the community, but the hard core remained. We were all a bit like George Fraser and Bob Rusk, two old prospectors who had for thirty years lived according to a fixed pattern on their claim at Paris on Dominion Creek. Paris had once been a small city of several thousand gold-seekers and had got its name because most of them were French-speaking. Now Paris consisted only of these two men. In the summer they washed out small amounts of gold. In the winter they vegetated. They subscribed to all the big magazines and during the warm months allowed them to pile up in a stack in their cabin. Then, when the snow fell, they sat down to read their way through them. By the time they were finished, the first robins were singing and it was time to start the water in the sluice-box again. From this routine they seldom departed. They had not been Outside since they first arrived in '98, and they rarely made the thirty-mile trip into Dawson. In fact they spent the final twenty years of their life without moving more than a few miles from their cabin. They lived vicariously in the pages of the *Saturday Evening Post* and *Maclean's*, reading about things they had experienced only by the proxy of those cardboard figures who inhabit magazine fiction.

This, in a sense, was our pattern, too. Our ways were governed to some extent by the inflexibility of those seasonal anniversaries upon which the calendar of the town was set. We were well aware of the inevitability of the river breaking up in May, and the frost coming in August. More than most North Americans, I think, we had become used to a certain precision in nature. It was perhaps natural then that we should unconsciously strive to maintain a similar fixed design in our own lives.

There were those who tried to challenge the pattern—nature's as well as the town's. I recall in particular three clergymen whom I knew and liked well. There was Mr. Fleming, who was sent up by the United Church and who was, to use a phrase of the day, "a live wire". He certainly tried to enliven the community, but with no great success. I am afraid we made a pun on his name behind his back and called him "The Flaming Youth". It was his idea, among others, to keep the children off the streets on Hallowe'en, by holding what he called a "jamboree", organizing them into one carefully disciplined group and taking them to the cinema. This worked out very well, but when Mr. Fleming moved away and the church was closed, the jamboree never took place again.

Then there was Mr. Bryne, of the Church of England, who also tried to change us. He started a Boy Scout and Wolf Cub pack, organized picnics, campfires, weiner roasts, pancake parties, father-and-son banquets, and boys' camps. It used to worry the bishop, who was certain that Mr. Bryne would lose a child in the woods during one of these activities. At the evening weiner roasts on the hills, which were a feature of Mr. Bryne's tenure, the bishop could be seen following carefully behind the multitude on the way back home, counting and re-counting all the children and clicking his tongue disapprov-ingly all the way down. All of these commendable activities petered out when Mr. Bryne left town. It was, as far as I know, his first parish. He had plunged into it full of eagerness and ideas. Shortly after leaving Dawson he left the Church and became a schoolmaster. Perhaps we were all too much for him.

Then there was Mr. Longshanks, another Anglican minister, whose stature was in direct contrast to his name. He was a tiny, pert Englishman and he did his best to buck the climate as Mr. Bryne and Mr. Fleming had tried to buck the town. Mr. Longshanks simply refused to wear overshoes. He had had no need of them before and he stubbornly saw no need for them now. He wore a pair of plain black Oxfords, light and beauti-fully polished. In vain, we told him what would happen if he didn't protect his feet and pay more attention generally to the Yukon winters. He brushed it all impatiently aside. Soon after he left Dawson on a stretcher, suffering from a fearful case of rheumatism.

The doctors and the dentists, the ministers and the teachers came and went as methodically as the migrating caribou. We had some very good doctors in Dawson, and also some very bad ones, but few of them seemed to stay for long. There was the doctor who looked at a pimple on my breast and told me I had cancer and would have to have the breast removed. I persisted in believing it to be a pimple and fortunately I was right. I have never had the operation. There was the doctor who examined my daughter, suffering from an attack of 'flu, and announced she had chronic heart trouble and would never walk again. For an entire week we lugged the child hither and thither, keeping her off her feet and wondering what in God's name to do. She finally solved it herself by refusing to be carried about a moment longer. We set her down and let her run about, and twenty-five years later she is running still. There was the doctor who gave Frank an injection for something or other and found out he had used the wrong drug. Frank turned blue. I hustled the doctor out of the house, piled blankets and hot-water bottles on Frank, whose teeth were chattering and whose whole body was racked by a terrible shaking, and finally brought him round. We continued to use that doctor. We had to. He was the only one in town.

There was also poor Dr. Nunns, who was a good doctor. The tragedy was that he, too, was the only one in town. This meant there was no doctor for the doctor. Dr. Nunns went down with acute appendicitis and, with the whole town watching helplessly, died without medical aid. From then on, doctors worked in pairs in Dawson City.

We had two dentists, but we had them only in the summer-time. In the winter the town was without dental care. Then one fall, Frank made a decision. He came home one day in a state of great excitement.

"I've bought Faulkner's tools. He's selling out."

"You've bought a set of dentist's tools? Are you out of your mind?"

"Not a bit of it. I thought I'd potter about with them in the winters. You remember I helped out a dentist in Granville years ago. Why, they even called me Doc."

He quickly cleared out his den, set up a dentist chair and drill, and before we knew it prospectors, Indians—yes, and bank managers, too—were waiting in the living-room for appointments. Frank, of course, had no licence and little training, but he was better than nothing in the dead of winter when a man had a toothache and needed quick relief. I soon found out to my astonishment that certain townspeople would hold off their dental work until winter in order to go to Frank. There may have been several reasons for this. He was a gentle sort of man and did his best never to hurt anybody. He also charged less than the real dentists. Again—and I consider this the most valid reason—he always gave a man a healthy slug of good brandy whenever he pulled a tooth.

Under the code by which we lived in the Yukon, personal popularity had nothing to do with wealth, position or social status. The most popular man in Dawson was neither George Black nor Joe Boyle, in his day, nor even Bishop Stringer. He was a teamster named Dan Coates, a large, expansive man with great white handlebar moustache, a florid face and a throaty chuckle which could be heard all over town. He sat on his wagon, hitching his huge bulk of a body about in the seat and passing the time of day with the people he passed. Everybody from gold commissioner to prostitute called him Dan.

Popularity in Dawson was based on the intangible business of being "a good fellow", a phrase that defies definition. Frank I think was not particularly popular, for example, for he was not the conventional good fellow. He hated to be slapped on the back. He used long and unusual words and he was keen on correct pronunciation. He and John Black used to spend long evenings in the front room comparing different local pronunciations, like a couple of professors of English. Frank also declined to wear a hat, and this tended to set him apart. In the winter, of course, he wore the conventional fur head-dress, but as soon as spring came he insisted on going hatless, even in the rain, or on his rare visits with me to church. This used to annoy John Black, who was conventional about such matters. "I wish you would use your influence with Frank and try to get him to wear a cap, at least," he used to say to me periodically. "You know, people are talking. They think he's putting on the dog." Needless to say, knowing Frank's stubbornness, I didn't bother to try.

People were always "talking" in the Klondike. On the long winter's nights they had very little else to do. If you wanted to be one of the boys you had to be interested in gossip, and this, too, set Frank apart, for he had absolutely no interest in tittle-tattle about his neighbours. It did not add to his popularity. In the winter, when work was slack at the office, the men would crowd around the hot-air register to dissect their fellow townspeople, but Frank would get bored and go off by himself to copy old mining records, or work on his maps of the creeks, which were forever occupying his spare hours.

And yet he was greatly respected and I think loved by the strange, tattered old men who came in regularly to renew their claims or check up on mining law. It was not until years later, when Frank died, that I learned something of this and began to hear stories of how he regularly lent them money and helped them in various ways. He certainly never told me. The townspeople, I imagine, considered him somewhat eccentric, for he played chess and talked about Einstein's theory and subscribed to the *Scientific American.* For that matter, I myself had thought him eccentric on our first meeting, though I never again felt so. The truth of the matter is that he was a shy, nervous, sensitive man, in spite of his varied careers in the mining camp and his early rough life in the Klondike. I remember once when the Fraternal Order of Eagles, of which Frank was a leading member, were holding their annual ball. It was Frank's task this year to mount to the stage and announce that refreshments would be served. Old John Black, his whiskers abristle, slid up beside me as Frank walked up the steps to perform this simple task. "At last!" J. B. said. "At last we'll have someone who understands the English language and who won't employ that confounded word 'lunch'." At this moment Frank spoke. He was terribly nervous. "Lunch is now being served in the lunch-room," he said, and beat a hasty retreat. I really thought J. B. would die of apoplexy on the spot.

This made Frank's actions on a certain winter's day the following year more than usually remarkable. He came home from the office for the mid-day meal and, in a voice which trembled with anger, told us all how a miner up the Klondike valley had been charged with shooting a cow moose, an offence punishable under the law.

"What they can't seem to get into their heads," Frank said, "is that the poor beggar was starving to death. He *had* to eat. It was him or the moose. The whole thing is a bunch of damned nonsense, if you ask me, and the trouble is he's not going to get a fair shake. There's only one lawyer in town and he'll be prosecuting. George Black is Outside or he'd take the case in a minute. They'll give him some rookie policeman who doesn't care a hang about the business and find him guilty. He'll have to pay a stiff fine for saving himself from starvation."

He pushed his plate back from the table, and said, half to himself: "If I knew anything at all about law, I think I'd have a shot at defending him myself. It's a damnable piece of nonsense."

"But you don't know anything about law, dear."

"No, perhaps not. Nor do the people who charged him, it seems to me. Anyway, under British justice, a fellow doesn't have to have a licence to defend a fellow man. Well, it's time to get back."

I watched him walk down the wooden sidewalk to the administration building.

"Children," I said. "I think your father is really going to defend that man."

I remembered the hesitant sentence about "lunch" on the stage of the A.B. Hall and shuddered a little to think of Frank in court.

He returned that night with a look on his face which was half sheepish and half triumphant.

"You went to court this afternoon, I'll bet."

"Yes, as a matter of fact I did. I got to thinking about it

and decided I'd have a shot at defending him. He was very grateful, you know."

"I'm sure he was, dear. Did you win?"

"No, no. Lost, of course."

"I'm sorry."

"Well, funny thing is that didn't seem to matter too much. The point was I think he got an adequate defence. Also, he really seemed to feel so much better about it when I offered to help him out. I mean, I think he felt somebody was on his side."

Which was all there was to it, except one small item. The following day a large parcel arrived at our door, tied in brown butcher's wrapping. It contained a giant haunch of meat.

"Moose," said Frank. A pause, and then he added drily, "Cow moose at that, I imagine."

Thus, punctuated by small dramas, the years in Dawson slipped by. Slowly, but inexorably, the town's population continued to leak away. John Black finally left after more than twenty-five years to return to his law practice and his family in New Brunswick. Shortly after this, the Stringers left for good. The bishop had been appointed archbishop of Rupert's Land, the second-highest post the Church of England had to offer in Canada.

The bishop's final function could only have taken place in the Klondike. It involved the wedding of Minnie Fidler, an old prostitute from the dance-hall days who had for years been living a quiet life as the common-law wife of one of her former patrons. She had grown quite domestic and in the later years began appearing regularly at the various community affairs. She occupied a box all by herself in the A.B. Hall, a dumpy little woman with a chalk-white face covered by a veil, and a splash of bright red hair. Finally, she decided to marry her friend, and this caused great excitement in the town. I remember our butcher with great glee showing off the enormous turkey ordered for the wedding supper and the confectioner exhibiting a gigantic tiered wedding cake.

At first Minnie, a Roman Catholic, asked her priest to tie the knot, but this gentleman refused on the grounds that somewhere in Europe Minnie had left a husband who might or might not still be alive. Also, he suggested, Minnie had been thoughtless about confession. As the only other religious body was the Anglican Church and its only priest then on duty the bishop himself, Minnie appealed to him. He was in a quandary. Should he stand firm on the fine points of Christian rubric and leave the woman and her paramour living in sin? Or should he interpret the law more broadly and perhaps, thereby, save two souls? He decided on the more charitable course, and married them, and indeed presided at the wedding supper, where, as the *Dawson News* reported next day, "a good time was had by all".

The couple took a house in the better part of town and repaired there for a honeymoon. A few mornings later the R.C.M.P. received an indignant call from the bride. "I want you to come down at once. You know that new woman who came to live by me? Well, she is not decent! You should move her away quick, see?"

As the years moved on, the North continued to exact its tribute, and hardly a season passed without a small tragedy being enacted in one or another of the cabins in the town or along the trail. I remember the wave of horror that crossed the town when Stewart Barnes died. He was an Oxford graduate and a Greek scholar who lived in a small cabin in the north end. He had come in during the rush, intending to stay one year, and had remained, like many others in Dawson, for a lifetime. He was fond of long, solitary walks and, because he was a poor mixer, the people thought him odd. He was really out of step with the country, virtually penniless, unable to make enough to leave. One morning they found his emaciated corpse lying across the bed of his little cabin. He had starved to death, too proud to tell his friends or to ask for help. Beside him was a diary describing in meticulous detail his last days and hours. There was no one of us that did not feel a sense of guilt, for nobody was knowingly allowed to go hungry in the North. Credit in every store and restaurant was unlimited—to everybody. No one could skip a debt by leaving the country, for anybody who owed money was turned back by the Mounted Police.

Another winter we had a murder. An old prospector was found bludgeoned to death in his cabin along the Klondike road. The murderer was trapped by a single clue that had a peculiarly Klondike flavour to it. The old man had been killed for his money, but his money consisted of banknotes of great age, which he had been hoarding carefully since the days of '98. When these old bills began appearing in the stores, the police were quickly able to trace their man. His name was Barney West. He was found guilty and hanged. It was the first execution in Dawson since that one, a generation before, that Robert Service had attended.

Like the dead man's hoarded banknotes, most of our pleasures and pursuits in Dawson were years behind the times. The radio was the rage Outside, but there were no radios in Dawson. There was nothing to receive and heavy atmospheric static made short-wave listening vitually impossible. Our films were up to five years old and sometimes older. We finally saw D. W. Griffiths's *Birth of a Nation* in 1929. We got short paragraphs of current news events three times a week in the four or six pages of the *Dawson News*, which meant that our main headlines were not more than two or three days old. We learned about the foundering of the dirigible R-101 within forty-eight hours, for example. But for an extended and detailed account of the current events we had to wait until the Outside newspapers were mailed in from Vancouver. This took two, three, sometimes four weeks.

Our popular songs were hopelessly out of date. They filtered into town a year or more after they had been sung to death Outside. We were probably the last people on the continent to go ecstatic over the Charleston and the Black Bottom. Everybody was drinking Coca-Cola, according to the advertisements in the magazines, but it had not yet reached us. As for fashions, we wore our skirts down when the rest of the world wore them up and we wore them up long after they had gone down again. It was the arrival of the first boat each spring that brought us our first glimpse of what was in vogue in the outer world. Down the gangplank one day in late May came Mable Cribbs, the chemist's wife, in a skirt around her ankles. How strange she looked—for ours were up to our knees. She was instantly the most stylish woman in town, for she had been Outside.

It was these things that helped to keep Dawson in its apparent state of suspended animation. One went Outside for a visit to find that the world had moved on. One returned next spring to find that Dawson had remained exactly as before. My parents' letters from Ontario took as long as six weeks to reach me, and the August Book-of-the-Month selection seldom got through before November.

The airplane was to change all this, in time, but airplanes like everything else were late in coming to Dawson. I remember the first one arriving in 1927, piloted by a young man who instantly became the hero of the town. It looked just like the 'plane in which Lindbergh had flown the Atlantic earlier the same year. It swooped into Dawson one winter's day and landed on skis on the Yukon ice as the entire town rushed to the river bank. I can still see several of the little half-breed children from the hostel reaching into the air with their hands as if trying to pluck the strange new bird out of the sky. The words *Queen of the Yukon* were inscribed in flowing script on the aircraft's cabin, and she had arrived to establish an airmail route. The *Queen of the Yukon* crashed into some trees shortly after that and was replaced by the *Queen of the Yukon II*. It plunged like a rock one cold day into the Stewart River, and that was the end of 'plane, pilot and airmail service. The mail came in by stage weeks later, rescued from the river bottom, each letter encased in a thick jacket of frost and ice.

We lived vicariously, as George Fraser and Bob Rusk did,

in the pages of the Outside magazines and in the thick catalogues from Eaton's and Simpson's, the great mail-order houses in eastern Canada. I did most of my shopping—food, clothing and household needs—from these thick, shiny volumes. With pencil in hand and tape measure handy I pored over the finely printed pages, racking my brains to determine the relative weights of long underwear, the comparative warmth of flannel versus homespuns, the advantages of gaiters over overstockings and felt boots over moccasins. If the sizes were wrong when the goods arrived we had to make do, for the distance was so great that it was impractical to return anything. There was no use sending back a child's dress because it was too large. By the time the replacement arrived it would almost certainly be too small. Thus we did our Christmas shopping in September and in November we had a miniature Christmas Eve, for that was when we had to wrap the parcels for friends and relatives Outside. Christmas itself seemed to run along for several days, for many gifts from the Outside would be late in arriving and for a couple of weeks after the Yule season they would still be trickling in on the Saturday stage.

It was not surprising then that the Great Depression, which began in 1929, should be almost three years late in arriving in Dawson. We had heard vague reports of bread lines and soup kitchens and mass unemployment Outside, but the Outside world was always a remote world, unconnected with our own world, where such news seemed hardly true. In the Yukon full employment and high wages continued on. And then, in the spring of 1932, the Depression began for us. I use this date because it was then that Frank was told he was out of a job. The Federal Government at Ottawa was abolishing the position of gold commissioner and reducing staff as an economy measure. At the age of sixty Frank was superannuated with a small pension.

Now we had a hard decision to come to. Should we remain in the Yukon or should we too, as so many had before us, quit the Klondike for good? The heart whispered "stay" but the mind urged "go", and it was logic, rather than sentiment, that we had to follow in the end. We would be able to scrape by with a pension in some small backwater of the Outside world, but it would not maintain us in the North, where prices were still sky high.

Thus, with the golden summer at its peak, we began to pack our bags and settle our affairs and prepare to leave Dawson for ever.

Seventeen

DISCOVERY DAY, 1932 . . . thirty-six years since George Carmack started it all on Bonanza Creek . . . twenty-five since I had first seen Dawson City. I was standing with the children, as we always did on Discovery Day, watching the Pioneers' Parade form up in front of the old log lodge hall on King Street, next door to Pantage's old Auditorium Theatre, an ornate wreck of slanting walls and gingerbread fretwork that looked like a piece of a Hollywood Western set. The Pioneers themselves fitted that set, for they all looked like Hollywood extras in their black suits and their big grey moustaches and their nugget chains dangling across their tight vests.

All day long, the people had been pouring into Dawson—trucks overflowing with crews from the dredges and construction camps on the creeks, old battered Model T's carrying miners and their families from Quartz and Last Chance and All Gold and Bonanza, canoes and motor-boats full of Indians from Moosehide, the squaws carrying their papooses securely tied on their backs and wearing coloured shawls and bright kerchiefs, the younger natives sporting the latest styles as shown in Eaton's catalogue, the streets a hurly-burly of dust and dogs, snarling, barking, playing, fighting and howling everywhere.

This was a day for nostalgia—our last Discovery Day in Dawson and Frank's last parade. Watching the greying men, as they adjusted the purple sash of their Order and formed up in a shambling line behind their banner, the memories of a quarter of a century in the North began to crowd across my mind like scenes in a newsreel. Each August 17 I had come down here to the Pioneer Hall to watch the parade start off and to follow it along the streets to the park. In the first few years, the parade stretched for many blocks and the men who paraded marched with a young, brisk step. Now the line of plodding men was hardly a block in length and the plodders were stooped and shambling. There was not a man in this parade who had not come into the Klondike before the turn of the century. These were the handful of stampeders who had remained after the fever died and the captains and the Eldorado kings departed. They had come up through the marshes of the Stikine and down the Teslin River, or up the ice steps of the Chilkoot and White Passes, or around by the Mackenzie and the Peel and over the Rat River Divide, or up the two thousand miles of river from the Bering Sea. None of them had found much gold. Most of them were content to lay their bones in the Yukon valley.

The line of men was beginning to move through the hot, white dust of King Street. They were walking on the very gravel—the famous "white channel" gravel of Lovat Gulch and Cheechako Hill—in which some of the most fabulous discoveries were made. Now the gravel, plundered of its gold, was used to pave the streets and avenues of the old gold camp.

I watched them come. There was Harry Francis, a teamster from new Brunswick, one of the three men with whom Frank had floated down the Yukon on a raft. He lived in a tiny, almost airless cabin attached to his stables on the south end of town. He had lived so long alone with his horses that he had taken on some of their attributes. He smelt slightly of stable manure and his clothes had a shapeless, colourless look. His tragedy still lay before him, on that bright August day. He had left a sweetheart behind when he left New Brunswick a young man, and she had promised to wait until he sent for her. A few years after this Discovery Day he did send for her, when both had reached old age. The call was forty years late in coming and when she arrived in Dawson, full of hope, she did not recognize the young man who had left her with a kiss to seek his fortune in the Klondike. The ageing teamster must have seemed to her like a strange, unsavoury animal. But she married him as she had promised and went to live with him in his cabin. The marriage did not last long. One spring day she vanished. Her steps could be seen freshly imprinted in the wet snow. They led straight as an arrow to the cold Klondike, and there they ended. A year or so later, the river claimed Harry as well. He was trying to cross the Yukon with his team when the ice gave way with a mighty crack and he and his horses went under, never to emerge.

The parade had reached Front Street and was now turning past the Yukonia Hotel, which used to be the M. & N. in the old days. Sam Bonnifield, the gambler, owned it once. He lost it on the turn of a card and won it back again, all in a single night.

Eddie Rickard came plodding by—Eddie Rickard, the soft-spoken, courteous old second-hand man who kept a shop on Front Street crammed with a curious collection of junk and knick-knackery which could have accumulated only in a deserted gold camp. Eddie always had something of everything. He had walking-sticks he carved himself from willows and aspens found along the Klondike valley. He had rusted gold-pans and soda siphon bottles and old calendars and curious old clocks from the gold-rush days. He had ashtrays made by himself out of old sardine cans and crockery found in miners' cabins and pictures of Landseer stags in ornate gilt frames. The only thing about Eddie was that he would never willingly sell any of his great collection. You could go in his store and bargain all day and Eddie invariably replied: "Well, now, I'm awful sorry, but I don't think I want to let that there go. It's the only one I got." A friend of mine saw a small hand organ in Eddie's shop which she tried to buy. Eddie refused to sell it. Thirty years later, when he died and his goods were sold at auction, she finally got it. For Eddie was one of those who dreamed of another boom. He had never quite emerged from the days of '98 when men made fortunes overnight speculating in just such commodities as he had in his shop. "Yessir," Eddie would say, a faint light in his eyes. "The boom's coming. I can smell her coming." But the boom did not come in Eddie's days. When he died finally and they sold his goods at auction they found something that surprised a lot of people. Eddie had left a will stipulating that out of the money realized from his stock a sum was to be set aside sufficient to buy a bottle of Scotch whisky at Christmas time for every indigent Pioneer in town, as long as he lived. The Government looked after these old men, but its charity did not extend to spirits. For this reason Eddie's name will be enshrined in Dawson long after those of his customers are forgotten. The old men are still drinking his whisky at Christmas time.

The parade was passing the Royal Alexandra Hotel now, and the steamer docks where both the *Casca* and the *Klondike* were berthed. It was a glorious August day, the leaves just starting to turn orange and yellow. A group of tourists were standing in front of the Royal Alex and they made way for the crowd of townspeople following the parade along the wooden sidewalks as it made its way to Minto Park in the centre of town.

I spotted Chris Fothergill in the crowd. He lived in a sod-roofed cabin just below our house. Somewhere on the creeks he had a claim which he spent most of his time working. He asked me to look up his family when I took the children Outside and I was happy to do so. They were pleasant farming people in Ontario and they were expecting Chris to arrive home for good any time. He sent them nuggets from time to time and they thought he was a wealthy miner. Somewhere he had a fiancée whom he always intended to marry but didn't. The Chris they talked of and the Chris I knew were different people. They spoke of a young man, affluent, urbane and vigorous, and I knew an old man, tired and hard-working and wealthy only in his memories.

The parade had turned up Queen Street towards Fifth Avenue, and I and the children followed along. Again my mind went back to the vigorous young men I had seen on Bonanza that day with The Bird, twenty-five years ago. Some of them were in the Discovery Day crowd today. There was Fred Elliott, a slender, white-haired Englishman from a wealthy family, who once lived in a house on Berkeley Square, where the rents were eight hundred pounds a year, and now occupied a one-room cabin on Dominion Creek. There was Red Ferguson, a tall, loose-jointed man with a fierce red beard now turning white, who worked on the dredges each summer and lived all alone in the north end during the winter. He spent all his time in the library, reading, reading, reading, but talking to nobody, a solitary figure in clothing that was always tattered.

There was Arthur Coldrick, still looking like a figure on the Strand, and there was Searle, grown old and white, his hopes still pinned on the Lone Star mine. There was Twa Donalds, still living in his spotless cabin on the hill above Dawson, and "Bull" Ballantyne, who once carried a load of two hundred pounds over the Chilkoot, and Grant Henderson, whose father told George Carmack where to look for gold.

There were the McKinnon brothers, Donald and Archie. How old they both looked, one of them almost blind! They were potentially worth tens of thousands of dollars, for they owned a group of claims on Indian River which they could not work but which they stubbornly refused to sell. They had had dozens of chances to sell, but had always balked at signing. T. D. MacFarlane once told me he had sat up an entire night wrestling with them, trying to persuade them to sell out to an English company for thirty thousand dollars and get some money for their old age. They wouldn't do it. Jock Spence, negotiating for a third party, spent days trying to get them to sell. "I'd rather live on oatmeal for the rest of my life," said Donald. Now here they were, still clinging fiercely to their property, and marching proudly with the others. A few years after this they both died in St. Mary's Hospital.

We were moving along Fifth Avenue now, the townspeople on the high wooden sidewalks, the Pioneers trudging along the gravel of the road. A float full of school children passed by with Dan Coates, his flowing moustache newly trimmed for the occasion, driving it, and passing the time of day with the people along the way. Behind was a wagon full of sourdoughs from St. Mary's Hospital, too old to walk. In and out between the vehicles and the marching men, the sons of the Pioneers were threading on bicycles gay with orange crêpe paper. It made a bright contrast with the grey men in the black suits and purple sashes.

Percy de Wolfe was in the parade that day. They called him The Iron Man of the North, and with good reason. Every winter Percy carried the mail from Dawson to Eagle, Alaska, by motor-boat, canoe, horse sleigh or dog team. He had travelled a hundred thousand miles on this eight-day, thrice-monthly trip, in snow, or blizzard, wind-storm or fifty below. Sometimes when the ice was breaking in the river he jumped from cake to cake with the mail sack on his back. Sometimes he took his gas launch through the shifting ice. Once his dog team went through into the freezing water and the lead dog dragged him to safety. The Iron Man never forgot that and when the dog finally died he brought his body into town and had Bill Strathie, the tinsmith, make a permanent metal coffin for him. Percy was known as a man who would protect the mail before he protected himself. Once he and his sleigh and three horses cracked through the ice. The horses were sucked under and drowned in a moment but the wagon box fell free and was slower to go down. Percy climbed up on it, slashed through the canvas cover with a knife and, waist deep in water, the box swirling in the river eddies, pulled out the twenty-two sacks of mail and flung them free. Then, freezing cold, he made his way four miles to the nearest road-house. Now here he was quietly trudging along with the rest of the men who came north with him more than thirty years before.

The parade had reached the Government buildings and was about to turn into Minto Park. Like everything else in Dawson, Minto Park too seemed strangely distorted. When they built it, it was flat as a billiard table, but the ceaseless heaving and settling of the frozen ground had turned it into hills and valleys and now it hardly looked like a park at all.

The last of the Pioneers were moving into the park. There was Chief Isaac of the Moosehide Indians. He had been in the North longer than any other Pioneer, for he was born here, and he wore his purple sash proudly. Stuck into his hat were several feathers, emblematic of his chieftainship, though I doubt if the Stick Indians, to whom he belonged, ever did wear feathers in the old days. There was Charlie Tennant, who also believed with Eddie Rickard that a boom was coming to Dawson. He had bought up every old cabin and shack and vacant lot in town, and if property meant wealth, then he was the richest man in town. There was George Black, looking dignified and reserved, as befitted a man of his new stature, for he had recently been appointed Speaker of the Canadian House of Commons. And there was Frank, on his last parade, keeping carefully in step. How he hated to be leaving the Yukon!

The parade wound into the park and broke up around the old bandstand, where George Black made the annual speech paying tribute to the men who had come over the pass years ago and to the pioneer spirit that built the country. It was, as it always was, a speech full of optimism, predicting a great future for Dawson City, and the listeners cheered as they heard it. I looked around me in the crowd. There was Kawakami, the little Japanese, still bright-eyed and eager-looking, but his face seamed and grizzled. There was Mme. Tremblay, who kept a dress shop. She was the first white woman to cross the Chilkoot Pass and she had been in the Yukon since 1894. And there was Jan Welzl, that curious Slovakian with the huge iron-grey Prussian moustache, who lived in the Holme Miller warehouse on Third Avenue, behind whose newspaper-draped windows he worked perpetually on a perpetual-motion machine. He had travelled from Czechoslovakia right across Russian Siberia to the Bering Sea and thence up the Yukon to Dawson —surely the longest route taken by any man to reach the

Klondike. There, not far from him, stood Klondike Rose, the deaf old prostitute who lived in a cabin along the Klondike River. She was one of the indigents to whom the I.O.D.E. used to send an annual Christmas parcel. (I remember she always insisted on pure woollen clothing.) I went to visit her on one of these occasions and we had a long talk. I asked her if she would like something to read, but she replied that she did not care for books. "Someone gave me a Bible once and I tried my best to read it," she said, "but I came on so many dirty stories that I closed it up and never opened it again."

The speech was over and the sports events began. There were races for the children and after that there was a baseball game. There were prize vegetables and home cooking and preserving to be judged and tea to be served in a tent and free soda pop for the youngsters. In the evening there was a dance in the A.B. Hall, and here for the last time we danced the minuet as we had in the days before our marriage so many years ago.

Thus passed our last Discovery Day in Dawson. In the days that followed I packed up those things we could afford to take with us and disposed of those that we couldn't. The packing brought back memories. Here was a pan I'd used to cook with during our honeymoon on Sourdough Gulch. Here was the frog costume that won Frank first prize at the New Year's Eve Ball. Here was the flag from the poling boat in which we'd floated down the Yukon.

A couple of nights before we left, Frank came home looking a little sad.

"Well, I've sold the *Bluenose*," he said. "A woodcutter bought her. He wants to take her downriver to do some freighting." He had put not only his skill but his very heart into this boat and I knew it was not easy for him to part with her. Some of our happiest days had been spent aboard her, lazing up and down the river in the warm summer evenings.

And Grey Cloud, now grown old and blind, had to be disposed of, too. He was too far gone to give away. Frank took him out to the woods late one evening, after the children had gone to bed, patted his head, settled him down into the leaves and shot him.

The following night we were walking home along the water-front when Frank stopped suddenly. "Listen," he said, and cocked his ear towards the river and the sound of a high-pitched motor. "There goes the *Bluenose*."

We waited quietly on the bank while the rhythmic sound drew nearer. "There she is," said Frank softly, pointing out into the main stream as the late-evening sun glinted on her blue prow. "She always did ride well, didn't she?" Automatically we turned to look for the dog, who whenever he heard the *Bluenose*'s engine rushed to the water-front. But the dog was gone.

The following day was our last in town. The house was sold, the boxes packed. As usual, the dock was crowded with people when we arrived to board the *Casca*, and again I recalled my first view of Dawson. The people on the dock were older now, but some of them were the same. Coming across Front Street I spied the familiar figure of Apple Jimmy, walking over from his shop, one hand outstretched in greeting, the other holding a bag of fruit. It was almost the identical scene that had greeted me twenty-five years before. Jimmy's hair had been black when he welcomed me that first day, his face as smooth as pock-marked skin can ever be. Now his head was quite white and heavy lines marked his brown, leathery face, but his black, quick eyes still sparkled, and his handshake, in good-bye, was as firm as it had been in welcome.

The final whistle blew and we boarded the *Casca*. As the sound reverberated around the Yukon hills, a husky began to howl in the weird, minor cadence of his breed. Another dog took up the howl, and another and another, until the mournful strain floated over the town, echoing across the deep bowl in the mountains, echoing over the grey roofs of the buildings and the flanks of the Midnight Dome, where red currants still grow thick in the summer, echoing over the west side of the river where the bones of the old ships lie, and up the Klondike valley where the tailing piles run for miles like miniature alps, and over those wooded river islands where we spent so many summer evenings.

The dogs were still howling when the boat passed the mouth of the Klondike River and chugged round the bend.